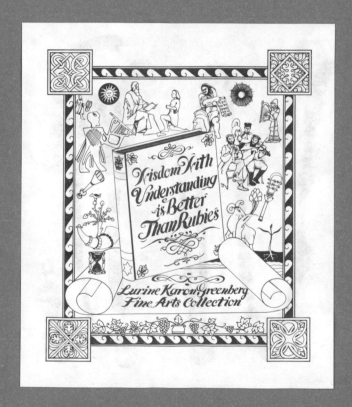

Gwathmey Siegel

Gwathmey Siegel & Associates Architects

Buildings and Projects

1992–2002

First published in the United States of America in 2003
by Rizzoli International Publications, Inc.
300 Park Avenue South, New York, New York 10010
www.rizzoliusa.com

Library of Congress Cataloging-in-Publications Data
Gwathmey Siegel: buildings and projects 1992-2002
edited by Brad Collins;
introduction by Robert A.M. Stern.
p. cm.
ISBN 0-8478-2529-9
1. Gwathmey Siegel & Associates Architects.
2. Architectural practice, International.
3. Architecture, Postmodern—United States.
I. Collins, Brad.
NA737.G948G83 2003   93-10438
720'.92'2—dc20   CIPs
2003 2004 2005 2006 2007 / 10 9 8 7 6 5 4 3 2 1

front cover: The New York Public Library, Mid-Manhattan Library, plan; Bel Air Residence, photo by Scott Frances
inside front flap: Naismith Memorial Basketball Hall of Fame, photo by Scott Frances
back cover: International Center of Photography, photo by Paul Warchol
inside back flap: San Onofre Residence, photo by Assassi Productions
residential divider (p 10-11): Malibu Residence: Second-level plan; View from northwest, photo by Erhard Pfeiffer
corporate divider (p 128-129): The David Geffen Foundation Building: Ground-level plan; View from southwest, photo by Tom Bonner
cultural & institutional divider (p 180-181): Levitt Center for Institutional Advancement: Fourth-level plan; Detail of rotunda, photo by Assassi Productions

Design and type composition by group c inc / New Haven (BC, SC)
Printed and bound in Hong Kong

Gwathmey Siegel

Edited by Brad Collins

Gwathmey Siegel & Associates Architects

Buildings and Projects

1992—2002

Introduction by Robert A.M. Stern

Preface

Design is a discovery process. It is a formal investigation of ideas and strategies that results in a work that transcends accommodation. As a process, it is essentially reductive and interrogative. If resolved holistically, the aesthetic is inherent and unreplicative.

The work presented in this volume documents this process as a sequence of investigations that informs all of our work. It is a process of growing, refining, and changing. We start with the residences because they are, at a certain level, formal and prototypical studies representing an ideal. They are ideograms and microcosms of an interpretation of architecture. They are laboratories for developing strategies that are universal rather than idiosyncratic. Ideally, they are paradigms.

Given the composite nature of this monograph, one can trace the development of certain ideas and strategies within one building type, and then decipher the influence of one building type on another as a continuous investigation of our process. Each project presents a set of clues; each is part of a process of sequential and incidental investigation that continuously infuses the work, resulting in revelations and extensions.

The development of ideas is cross-time and cross-typology. There is, in principle, no separation between the investigation of the house and the investigation of a museum or an office building. In our mind, it is all architecture, and it is all a process to enrich and refine and, ultimately, create an essence that resolves a particular problem in a particular place.

Our work is always a speculation of the incomplete.

Introduction

1

2

3

After thirty or more years of busy practice, Charles Gwathmey and Robert Siegel have not only remained true to their ideals but have also been endlessly inventive in realizing them. They have not reduced or repeated, but revised and enriched.

What can one add to the interpretation and appreciation of work that has so successfully and so uncompromisingly stayed the course of its initial intentions for a generation? Clearly these architects have a point of view that has resonated with the public and with patrons. They know what they are doing and, quite rightly, they are widely appreciated for their gifts to the art of architecture.

Given this, what I am writing is purely superfluous: the partnership of Charles Gwathmey and Robert Siegel needs no introduction; the work, in its tectonic clarity, spatial inventiveness, and programmatic integrity surely speaks for itself. It has its own distinct personality—a personality that was fully formed at a very early stage of their partnership. When they found their voice, these architects were younger than any of us in our shared generation. Their early maturity was daunting. Over the years their ability to grow while remaining in touch with their origins has not only been admirable but also awe-inspiring. With Charles Gwathmey's house for his parents in 1966 [1], the direction of this practice was set — the crystalline geometry, spatial invention, and meticulous construction of that house was the beginning of an arc of exploration that continues to this day, describing a line of pursuit that continues to hold the partners' interest and ours as well. Of course there have been changes in the practice — it began with houses, and was quickly bolstered by residential and commercial interiors. Later came office buildings, libraries, and museums. No matter the building type, but especially in the smaller and medium-sized program-intensive buildings which are their forte, the consistency of quality, attention to detail, and sheer invention over the years is amazing. This is not to say that these architects have not repeated themselves. What artist in any art has not? Nor have they worked in isolation from prevailing trends. What artist can or indeed should? The early work of Le Corbusier has been their guide, but they have not been imprisoned by their master: he has not bound them to his vision in the way he has others of our generation. Gwathmey Siegel have seen in Le Corbusier not only compositional strategies and specific tropes of plan and section; they have also seen a sensuousness of shape and color and texture that has eluded most others who have also taken him as master. As a result, especially in their interiors, they have frequently surprised us with a softer, more romantic approach than their early work led us to expect.

There is another powerful architectural influence at work, which perhaps explains why the influence of Le Corbusier, though almost never absent in the work, is never tyrannizing. That other architectural influence is Louis I. Kahn. Charles Gwathmey first learned of Kahn while an undergraduate at the University of Pennsylvania, and transferred to Yale to study with him — only to find that his would-be master had quit New Haven for Philadelphia. Be that as it may, Kahn's presence can be felt in the work: in the bold geometries exploring elemental shapes, and even more so in the tectonic clarity of the work. Le Corbusier was a painter-architect; but Kahn was a constructor, whose every building was considered in terms of specific materials selected, and construction techniques pursued and explicitly expressed. That sense of architecture as a builder's art is central to the work of Gwathmey Siegel and quite apart from most other work by contemporaries.

Houses are the firm's stock in trade, the base case of their creativity, and when they've tackled other, larger, less spatially varied building types, they have sometimes seemed sidetracked. In the 1980s Gwathmey Siegel designed office buildings, including one notable addition to Midtown Manhattan's skyline, 1585 Broadway [2], but more typically suburban examples in New Jersey and along the freeway leading to Intercontinental Airport in Houston [3]. In these, their artistry was principally confined to the external envelope which they organized with a two-dimensional patterning that reveals deep knowledge of graphic design. They have also taken on the vexing problem of the college residence hall. Part hotel, part monastery, and almost always underfunded, the residence hall has been the bête noire of many Modernists. When we were students, Philip Johnson, Charles Gwathmey's teacher and mine, admonished us to treat with respect those top architects who could survive this very hard building type over which Breuer, Johnson, and Saarinen had stumbled. Gwathmey Siegel was put to the test very early on in their career at the State University of New York's Purchase campus of 1972 [4], and a few years later at Columbia [5] where they attempted to synthesize the height and density of a late twentieth-century Corbusian block with the collegiate cloister of an earlier, gentler time. Neither building was completely resolved, but each was head and shoulders above the simple-minded diagrams that our teachers' generation had offered by way of example.

While the work of Gwathmey Siegel has been described as self-referential in formal language, and object-fixated in composition, in recent years, the scope of their explorations has grown to include a more nuanced approach that, though not explicitly contextual in the Post-Modern sense, is nonetheless deliberately and distinctly embedded in the specifics of place. Their addition to Frank Lloyd Wright's Guggenheim Museum [6], one of the most complex of the firm's undertakings, from the technical, symbolic, and political points of view, was a project of the late 1980s that can be said to have introduced this new site-specific dimension to the work. It can be seen more clearly in the village-like massing of the Zumikon residence [7] which nestles into its Swiss hillside or in the Henry Art Gallery at the University of Washington in Seattle [8], where the building burrows into the berm-like campus edge and breaks apart to allow for connections to older parts of the museum and cross-connections between different parts of the campus. In each of these projects, the strong imagistic or iconic identity of the new building, a hallmark of so much of Gwathmey Siegel's work, plays second fiddle to the idea of the site, one quite rural or at least suburban, the other a densely built-up campus. But once inside these two buildings, the light-filled volumes, the overlapping synergies between spaces of passage and those of repose characteristic of almost all of their work, is very much present.

Interestingly, the firm's first exploration of the embedded building type was also for a museum: Werner Otto Hall, housing the Busch-Reisinger Collection at Harvard University. Squeezed onto a tight site bounded by the Georgian-style Fogg Museum and Le Corbusier's sculptural jeu d'esprit, the Carpenter Center for the Visual Arts, Werner Otto Hall, despite its literal embeddedness, comes off as a distinct, some would say too distinct, entity. Yet it is a very sympathetic setting for the collections it displays, as are all of the firm's museums. Unlike so many contemporary museums that swamp their contents with the sheer spectacle of their being, Gwathmey Siegel's are consistently, I would say insistently, sympathetic to the works of art on display. Creating sympathetic settings for art is probably second nature to Charles Gwathmey, son of two artists.

Most of this book is devoted to realized work—projects of the 1990s—which now seems almost another world away, not because of the millennium, which proved itself a non-event, but because of September 11, 2001. Among the very many architectural consequences of that day has been the onset of an adverse economic climate that threatens to stop projects conceived in the euphoria of the booming economy of the years leading up to it, including, it seems, Gwathmey Siegel's proposal for the New York Public Library's Mid-Manhattan Branch [9]. With its sensuous glass-clad shape slipped into and extending above the tight box of a conventional stone-clad mercantile palazzo, the design of the Mid-Manhattan library seems at first glance a new departure for the firm. But a closer inspection reveals the design not as a new departure but as a new development of one of Gwathmey Siegel's earliest projects involving the reuse of an old building—that is, the 1970 renovation of the fire-damaged Greek temple-like Whig Hall at Princeton [10]. Restating an idea in a new way, the Mid-Manhattan library holds out the promise of fresh but consistent work yet to come.

For Charles Gwathmey and Robert Siegel, Modernism is not a matter of taste, as it is for many who now, looking to the recent past nostalgically, treat it largely as a revival or a return, resulting in a kind of Post-Modern Modernism. For Charles Gwathmey and Robert Siegel it is something else, something more fundamental: it is a continuing exploration. Their work is not reviving anything, or ironically commenting on anything. Their work is about continuing, about adding new accomplishment to what went before. Seasoned masters, they go forward with the voice of experience and with the authority of intelligence, talent, and belief.

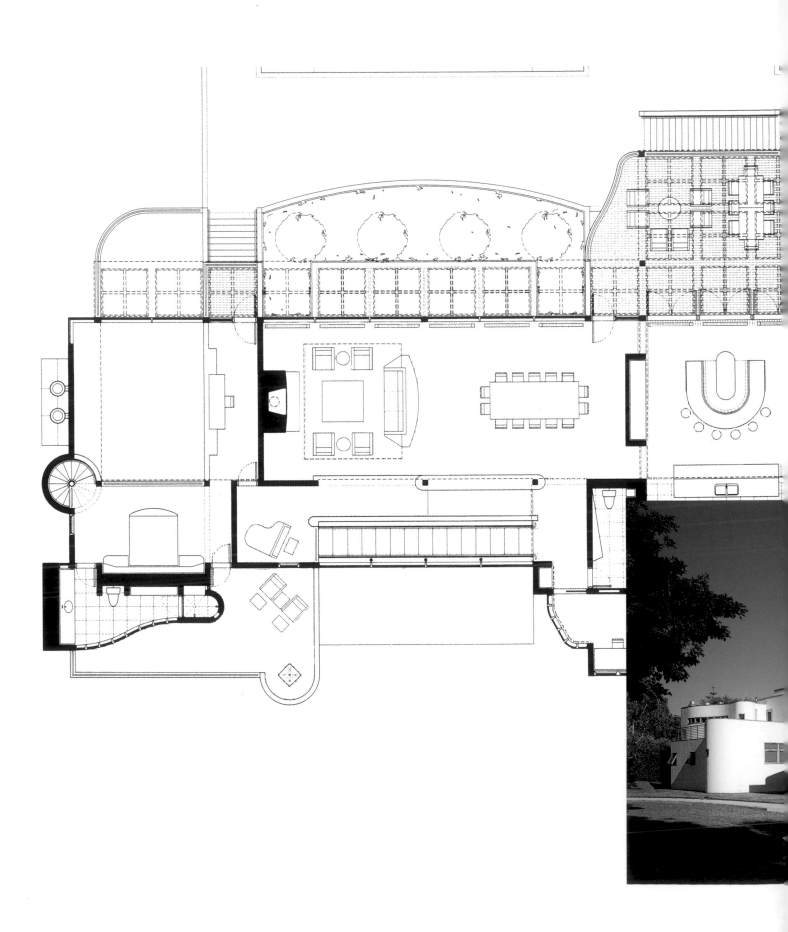

Residential

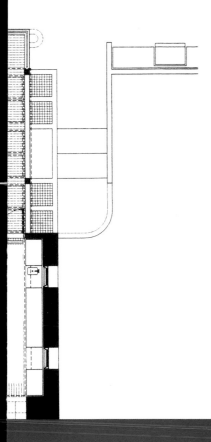

South façade

Zumikon Residence

During the design of this house our priority was to create a relationship to the site that integrates the architecture into the terrain in such a way that both create a harmonious entity.

Inspired by roof silhouettes, village squares and gardens, the house is divided into four related building elements. Each of these elements is self-sufficient, supporting the idea that the composition as a whole is a microcosm of a village.

The first of the four elements is the front building, located near the street, consisting of the entry, garage, kitchen/breakfast room and guest room. Its upper floor connects the service entry area to the second building element, the large terrace. This exterior space has two levels and integrates the swimming pool. The terrace is the heart of the house and can be conceptually compared to a "village square."

The third element of the house consists of a gallery and dining room, above which is a roof garden with a sculpture terrace. This roof terrace is the most important connection between the front and back elements of the building.

The fourth element, the main house, located at the rear on the sloping site, encompasses the living room, library, master bedroom, studio and "children's house," the forms and roofs of which are articulated in such a way that the parti of the village is reiterated formally.

The arrangement of the elements and their composition is directly related to the natural topography of the site. The grouping of interconnected building elements and exterior spaces integrates completely into the existing context and consequently enters into a sympathetic dialogue with the natural environment and the town.

Entering the house, one encounters a linear columned gallery that connects the two and one-half story front entry hall to the rear stair. The front stair connects the lower entry level to the main living level, one story above. The entry space establishes, under a curved, segmented roof form, the volumetric aesthetic of the house.

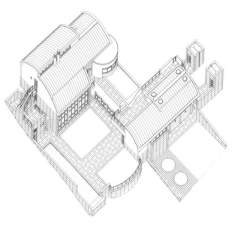

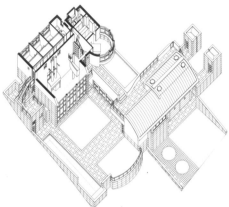

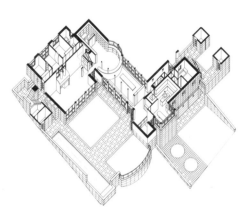

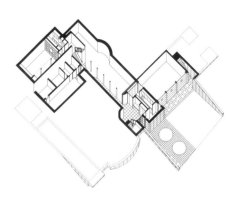

Roof-, third-, second-, and lower-level axonometrics | View from service court | Detail of south façade | Detail of east façade   Detail of east façade

Gallery from entry hall

The entry space engages one vertically and horizontally—vertically in section, with the entry stair balcony and upper roof, and horizontally, through the gallery to the back stair—revealing the diagram of the house. The horizontal connection is always land-driven and the vertical connection is always view-driven.

As the house engages the land and steps up the hill, horizontal spaces are created—a series of pavilions that are interconnected rather than consolidated. The conscious vertical manipulation of floor planes allows one space to overview another.

On the second floor, the dining room serves as a transparent mediating space between the natural topography of the fields to the east and the man-made courtyard/roof terrace to the west. The glassblock floor (which brings natural light into the art gallery below) and the concrete columns articulate the circulation zone.

A three-story cylindrical form, which is sliced and eroded, marks the intersection of the horizontal pavilion and the main house. The cylinder contains the terminal space of the gallery on the ground floor, the music room/library (overlooking the dining room) on the second floor, and the master bedroom on the third floor

Rotated from the music room/library, the double-height living space meets the intersection of the rear stair and horizontal gallery, and opens toward the main terrace and the view of Lake Zurich and the Alps beyond. The interior space is in scale with both the terrace and the view. Its back wall, which accommodates the fireplace—a sculptural anchor to the space, both wall-engaged and floating, an alternative focus to the view across the terrace—is also the front wall to the children's domain, another distinct element of the program, integrated into the composition but accessed as a separate vertical building.

Off the master bedroom, the roof of the dining room becomes a garden terrace, planted with annual flowers. It reestablishes, in the modernist tradition, the connection between occupied land and the building. This area is part of an integrated circulation system of terraces and outdoor spaces that bring one from the lower street-level entry court up through the three levels of the house.

The opportunity to build this house of reinforced concrete, given the level of craft that exists in Switzerland, was compelling and influenced the form. This is literally a building of the ground, with a density and sense of permanence that is entirely different from that of our wood-frame houses. The curved, segmented roofs are an elemental description of the volumes as well as a representation of the parti.

The materials used in this house—stucco on terra cotta for walls; lead-coated stainless steel for roofs; wood for windows and cabinetry; and limestone, sandstone, and wood for floors—produced a selective aesthetic so precise and hierarchical that it establishes the primary reading of the building and creates spaces that are inherently self-decorative.

Pool from upper terrace

Pomerantz Apartment

NEW YORK, NEW YORK

This apartment represents the transformation of a traditional 2,300 square foot Manhattan apartment into a spatially complex modern loft. Assymetrical interventions create dynamic spatial tensions that counterpoint the original structure and frame.

The apartment includes living, formal dining, eat-in kitchen, study, library, master bedroom suite with two dressing rooms, two bathrooms and a laundry.

Three exposed, round columns support the expressed, pre-existing beamed ceiling which acts as a "parasol" over the new plan and section.

The limestone floor, cabinets and bathroom walls are rotated from the orthogonal plan, reinforcing the object/frame strategy. The cabinets that enclose the study and the dressing rooms are capped with glass clerestory windows and "float" below the ceiling, ensuring privacy while maintaining spatial continuity

The undulating fireplace wall is "carved-away," revealing depth, and a sense of density. The fireplace is treated as both a traditional object—a central figure in the apartment—and a modern one, a sculptural juxtaposition with a manipulated wall surface.

The materials are limestone; maple and carpeted floors; integrally colored veneer plaster and back-painted glass walls; perforated stainless steel and; pearwood cabinets with granite, limestone and onyx tops.

Elevator entry hall | View from entry gallery   Detail of entry gallery

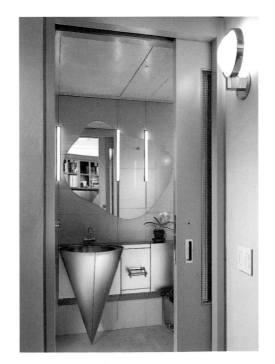

San Onofre Residence

PACIFIC PALISADES, CALIFORNIA

This private residence is located on one and a half acres at the end of Malibu Canyon. A bilateral parti derived from the site's unique profile—the majesty, stillness, and density of Malibu Canyon in contrast with the sun-drenched horizon of daytime and the city lights at night—afforded an opportunity to design two distinctly different elements and combine them into a consolidated architectural collage.

In addition to the two house structures, a third element— the site building, created by extending the two horizontal planes at different levels— involved constructing massive retaining walls (with caissons extending 65 feet to bedrock) and provided a unique opportunity for site integration and building organization. If one removed the house from the land, the retaining walls would be a formally resolved composition, as well as a transformed ruin.

A three-story curved limestone "pavilion" housing the main living spaces is poised on a promontory looking south and east toward Santa Monica, the Pacific Ocean, and the skyline of downtown Los Angeles. The pavilion, an object on the ground, is anchored and stabilized by the "canyon house," designed as a building in the ground. Separate, unique, and contrapuntal in its organization and its materiality, the pavilion, with its curved limestone wall, transforms the experience of the landscape as one moves through it from the ordered programmatic distribution of the canyon house.

The canyon house, organized vertically and bilaterally, contains the exercise room, bar, screening room, and library on the ground level; the children's bedrooms and garage on the entry level; and the office/conference suite, master bath, and dressing rooms on the third level, with its connecting bridge to the pavilion.

The core of the pavilion, housing the master bedroom on the upper level and the kitchen on the entry level, floats within the limestone perimeter wall. It is an object in a frame, a fragment of the canyon building that has been extended, forming the complex volumetric element that separates the double-height living and dining spaces. The breakfast room penetrates the screen of the brise soleil on the south glazed façade and creates an outdoor terrace extension off the master bedroom above.

The sequential unfolding of the site begins upon entering the house through a link element. Whether one enters on the main level or on the lower ground level, views of the canyon through the stair, and of the ocean through the pavilion, are immediately revealed, as well as the site integration and the intersection of the stair and the bridge reconciles the vertical and horizontal connection of the two elements. The link is the volumetric lock.

Detail of south façade   Lower ground-level entry terrace | Exterior stair connecting ground and lower ground-level terraces | Lower ground-level entry gallery

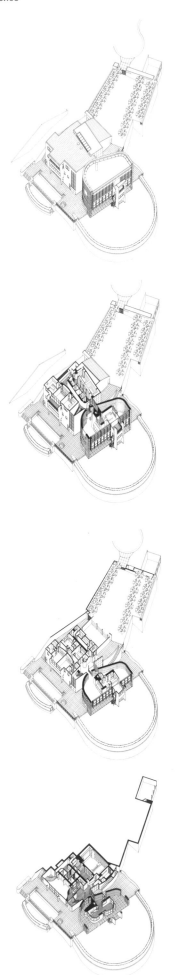

Master bedroom

Detail from southwest

West façade and Santa Monica from pool terrace

Winnick Apartment

NEW YORK, NEW YORK

This 2,000 square foot apartment is located in one of New York's venerable residential hotels at the southeast corner of Central Park.

The architectural transformation was accomplished by reconfiguring the space to exploit the views, creating a vista from the front door to windows looking north over the park. The living/dining space is conceived as a "loft" which is mediated by the intervention of the white glass cube, containing the study/guest bedroom.

The gridded, wood paneled, east wall of the entry gallery, defining the loft space, accesses the master bedroom suite and kitchen.

The material palette of grey sandstone, cherry and maple floors, steamed beech and cherry cabinetwork and paneling, stainless steel, white and patterned glass, and integral plaster walls and ceilings, afford a rich reference for a twentieth century art and furniture collection.

Entry gallery toward living

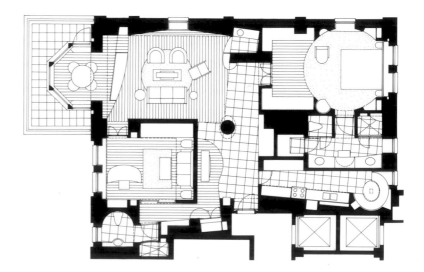

Living toward entry gallery

Malibu Residence

MALIBU, CALIFORNIA

This design represents a composite summary of our house investigations, instigated by a restrictive zoning code, a complex program and a spectacular three acre bluff site, overlooking the Pacific Ocean.

The site, accessed from the north through a tree lined drive on the west edge, provides an axial framed view of the ocean as well as the north façade of the house. The tennis court and guest house are located on the north portion of the site and the house and pool terrace on the south at the edge of the bluff. An extended lawn, the horizontal landscaped plane on which the building elements are placed, is a reinterpretation of the found object/frame strategy.

A longitudinal stair/ramp volume articulated by a major window wall and reflecting pool is the primary volume on the north entry façade. The entry gallery initiates the circulation sequence at the ground level which accommodates two children's bedrooms, guest bedroom, playroom and garage and continues below grade to the screening room and skylite gymnasium.

The first half-level accesses the double height sitting room, with a sleeping balcony above. The second level accesses the living/dining/kitchen/deck "loft." The split level parti is consolidated beneath a continuous inverted barrel vaulted roof defining the primary living spaces on the first half and second levels.

The integration of the generic modern double height volume and balcony, with the pavilion loft space, under the single roof form combines referential plan and section partis, resulting in a complex, yet unified three dimensional composition.

View from entry gate

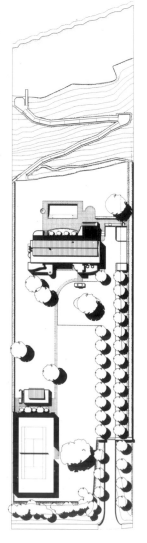

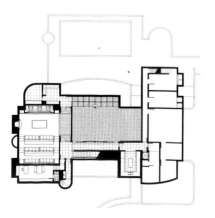

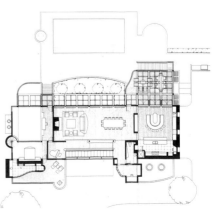

Detail of south façade | Exercise room

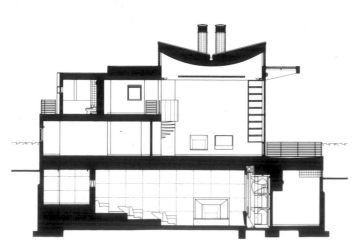

Stair from sitting room landing | Cross section through screening/billiard room, sitting, and master bedroom loft

Gymnasium Apartment

NEW YORK, NEW YORK

This 6,000 square foot apartment is located in the former gymnasium of the original Beaux Arts, New York City, Police Headquarters Building.

The intention was to physically maintain and visually exploit the volumetric integrity and structural expression of the existing barrel-vaulted space, while adding a master bedroom suite and study/library balcony, and integrating an eclectic painting and sculpture collection.

On the main level of the twenty-five foot high, steel-trussed volume, is the multi-use living/dining/entertainment/gallery articulated by custom designed, space defining furniture. At the east end of the space is the master bedroom suite, and study/library balcony accessed by an exposed stair, which rotates at the landing and runs parallel to and behind the existing longitudinal steel truss to attic guest bedrooms over the kitchen, master baths and dressing rooms.

The study/library balcony is suspended under the east end of the barrel vault and revealed from the master bedroom below, by a continuous radial skylight in the floor, articulating its separation while maintaining the volumetric extension.

The floor of the balcony defines the bedroom ceiling, floating asymmetrically within the existing orthogonal building frame, articulating its objectness and sectional variation.

Three large skylights were inserted into the south side of the barrel vaulted roof, providing natural light into the longitudinal internal façade of the space and revealing the "classic" building pediment above.

Living/dining

Living/dining from study balcony | Dining | Detail of stair

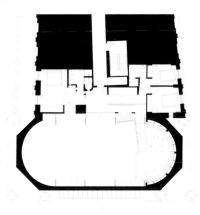

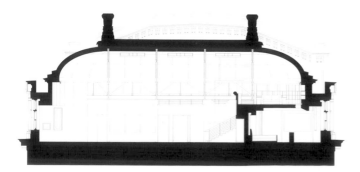

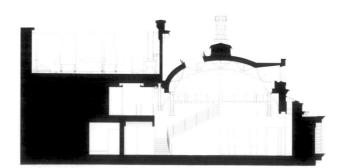

     Upper-level gallery toward study balcony, living | Longitudinal section | Cross section

Miranova Penthouse

COLUMBUS, OHIO

The opportunity to design a "house on the roof" of a new apartment building in downtown Columbus, adjacent to the river, with panoramic views and a major modern art collection, was unique.

The entry floor is organized around a modulating circulation/gallery space separating the double height living volumes, with their views, from the service spaces and building cores.

A 100-foot long wedge shaped triangular skylight, traversing two thirds of the plan, releases the roof to the sky and floods the interior with natural light, balancing the two story high glass perimeter walls, and adding a dynamic, volumetric, referential, iconic form to the space.

The program specified a library and private office suite, living space, formal dining space, kitchen/dining/family room, exercise space and spa, master bedroom suite, three guest bedroom suites, a sculpture terrace and gallery.

The entry gallery, accessed from the north elevator lobby adjacent to the two-bedroom guest pavilion, opens to the sculpture terrace and extends the circulation procession to the family spaces which are revealed sequentially.

The second level, accessed by two stairs, one from the living and the other from the family room, accommodates the master bedroom suite, with its balcony terrace overlooking the city and river, and a guest bedroom suite, with a balcony sitting area over the library.

The counterpoint between wall and glass, solid and void, establishes a dynamic and hierarchal layering of space which is simultaneously enriched and reinforced by the integration of the art collection into the architecture.

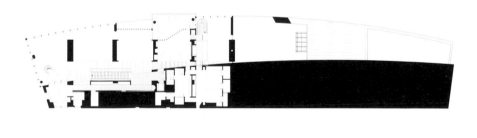

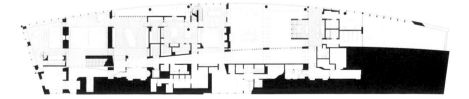

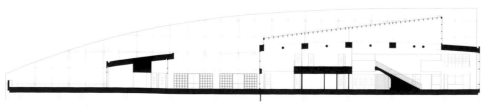

The 3,800 square foot duplex apartment in the iconic Beresford Building on Central Park West represents a total transformation of the traditional building topology.

The resultant "loft" is a sculpted, volumetrically manipulated, spatially dynamic environment.

The primary frame is rendered in integral plaster, while the private spaces are defined in wood, separated from the ceiling by glass clerestory transoms that reinforce the overall spatial continuity, while allowing for counterpointal, hierarchical intervention and programmatic specificity.

The material palette of stone and dark stained oak floors, stainless steel, titanium, anegre wood paneling and cabinet work, reinforce the spatial hierarchy and complexity, as well as establishing a sense of density and permanence.

The design fulfills the formal, object/frame strategy through a complex and composite layering that is both visually and psychologically resolved.

Dining toward kitchen   81

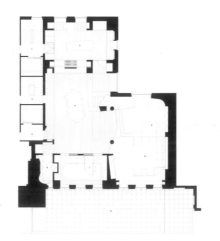

Steel Loft

The goal with this apartment was to perceive the "idea" of a single 4,400 square foot rectilinear volume, which is hierarchically modulated and articulated through the layering, horizontally and vertically, of the forms and space. The space, 110 feet long by 40 feet wide, has fourteen (seven pair) of south facing windows on the seventh floor of a loft building in Chelsea.

A line of existing columns, 18 feet from the south façade, articulates the main circulation gallery. A second circulation zone, visual and actual, parallel to and along the south window wall, accesses more private spaces—study, master bedroom suite, and master bath—through a sequence of thick wall niches that accommodate sliding steel and patterned glass doors for privacy.

The ceiling height to the underside of the slab is 9'10". Existing beams form a second ceiling layer and are the primary referential horizontal graphic through the entire space. Three ceiling/wall heights below the beams establish datums for primary and secondary walls, which do not engage the ceiling, but float below exaggerating the illusion of a higher space. These varying ceiling heights afford opportunities to conceal ambient indirect lighting as well as air-conditioning ducts and grilles, and preserve the overall spatial continuity.

The loft is a three-dimensional reinterpretation of a Mondrian; it is an architecture that is at once articulate, graphic, sublime, and calm. It is a space conceived as an "excavation," a carving away that results in an essentialness that is inherently sculptural—light filled, dense and sequential, where nothing is added or redundant.

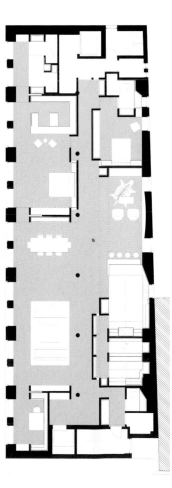

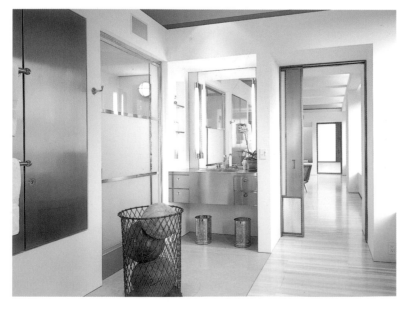

Master bedroom | Master bath | Master bedroom

View from study

EINSTEIN'S
1912 MANUSCRIPT
ON THE
SPECIAL THEORY
OF RELATIVITY

West façade from auto court

Hilltop Residence

Located on a previously undeveloped, wooded, eighty-five-acre site with views of the lakes, downtown Austin, and the University of Texas, this residence is programmatically unique in that it consolidates two distinct requirements in a single building—a "family house" program and an independent "entertainment" program, with extensive on-site parking to accommodate large family gatherings and business functions. The resolution of these two programs establishes the scale of the building and was critical in generating the parti.

The building is organized around a horizontal spine, with the "family house" and the "entertainment house" designed as complex figural objects integrated into the landscape and anchoring the two ends. The spine, as well as being the primary circulation element, is programmatically dense and is the site anchor.

The automatic response to the site would have been to place the building on the top of the hill. Instead, like San Onofre, it is both in and on the land. We created a full story grade change by building a plateau on the eastern portion of the site. The spine becomes a thick retaining wall, mediating between the existing, lower-grade entry level and the raised, private family level of the site. The house and the topography are integrated, simultaneously transforming the perception of the landscape and the architecture.

The composition is complex, fragmented, and collage assembled. It is read and understood sequentially rather than simultaneously. Forms are rendered as objects within an overall framework, and the fragmentation reinforces the composite as well as layered strategies. The material palette has been extended to further articulate volumetric and planar hierarchies. The base, engaging the grade, is granite; the primary walls are stucco, counterpointed by stainless steel panels and zinc standing-seam roofs and object elements. The interior materials are maple, cherry, limestone, and slate floors; pearwood cabinets, doors, and bases; and integral plaster walls and ceilings.

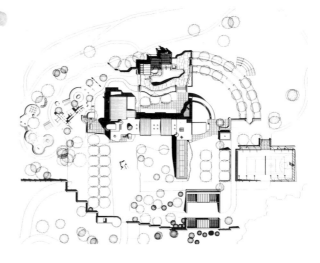

Site plan   93

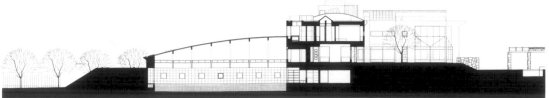

West façade toward natatorium | Cross section

Lap pool | Detail from southwest | Longitudinal section

Detail of entertainment pavilion

Pool terrace and pavilion from balcony | Entertainment pavilion with tent from pool terrace

Entertainment pavilion with tent and library from upper-ground-level terrace

North façade

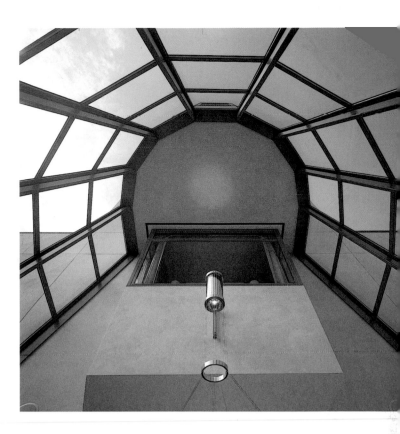

Living to third-floor study balcony | Dining to gallery | Family room to kitchen

Bel Air Residence

BEL AIR, CALIFORNIA

The buildable site, an existing two-acre plateau set sixty feet below the access road, affords panoramic views of Westwood, the Pacific Ocean, and the Stone Canyon. The program, orientation, and topography provoked a composite courtyard parti, that layers the site through the house, integrating the terraces and lawns.

The primary volumetric element of the house—orienting south, west, and north—accommodates the entry gallery, sitting room and living room on the ground level; two offices and sitting balcony on the second level; the master bedroom suite and deck on the third level. The screening room, bar/game room and garage occupy the lower level.

The linear/spine element accomodates the dining room, kitchen/breakfast room, and staff apartment on the ground level; the play room and three children's bedrooms on the second level; and a guest suite, exercise room and a massage room on the third level.

The sauna building/guest house, as well as the pool and terrace, are located on the eastern portion of the site, extending the outdoor spaces and completing the overall site-building design strategy.

Compositionally and formally, this house presents the most articulated, hierarchal, and consolidated plan graphic to date, which is further reinforced by its volumetric resolution. The primary sculptural element is the reverse cone at the west end of the circulation spine that anchors and orients the house to its site as well as to its primary interior spaces.

The massing and solid/void articulation is read as reductive, or the result of carving from an initial solid, rather than additive or assembled, giving the house a density and sculptural presence akin to the earliest beach houses.

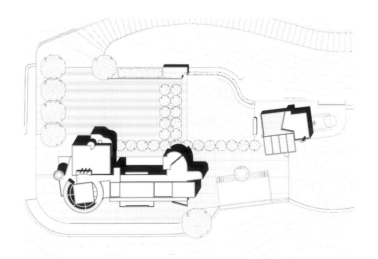

West façade

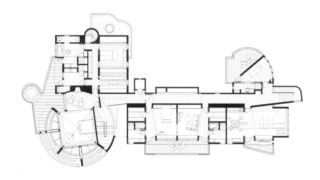

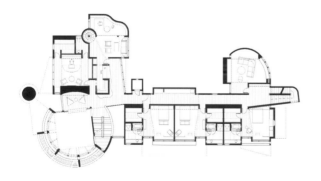

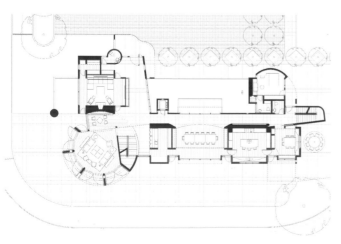

View from northwest | Third-, second-, and ground-level plans

Pool, terrace toward east façade

Pool toward guest house | Northeast from guest house deck

Detail of north façade from entry | Dining

Detail of north façade, entry

Living

Entry gallery toward stair, living

Stair from second-level gallery

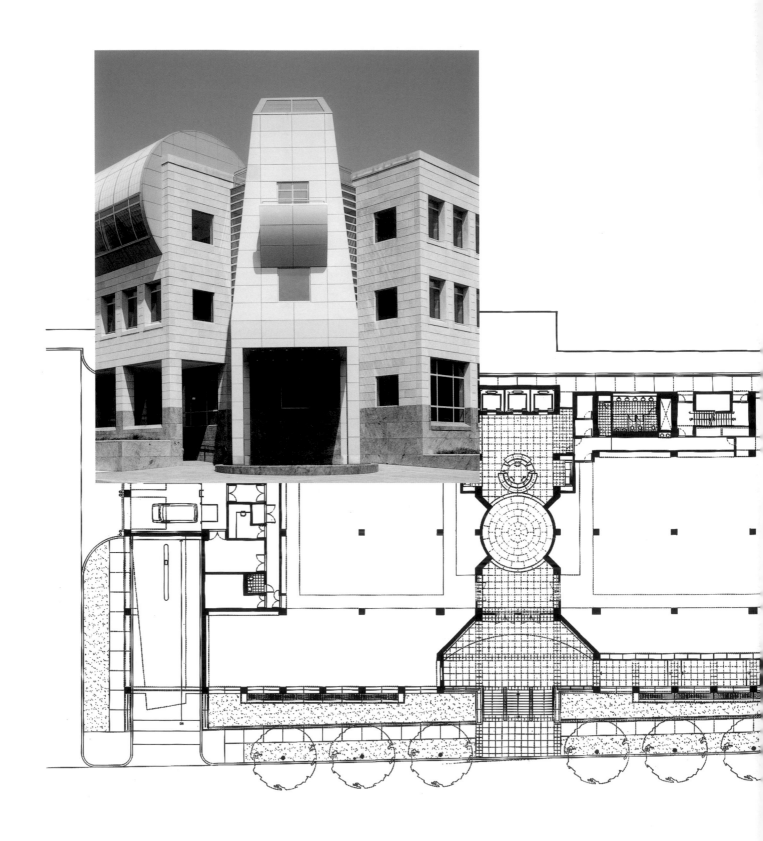

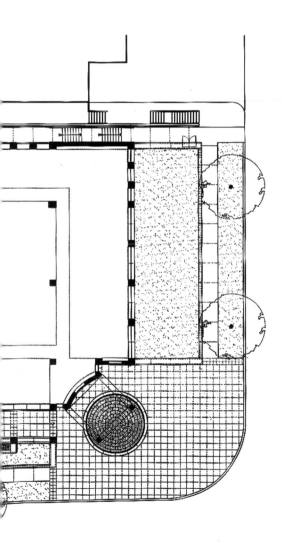

Corporate

Morgan Stanley World Headquarters

The design of this fifty-two story, 1.3 million square foot office building, located on the west block front of Broadway between 47th and 48th streets, reflects the dual aspirations of skyscraper tradition: to present a memorable skyline silhouette and an appropriately scaled public/pedestrian base.

The composition responds to the primary orthogonal Manhattan grid in the town, and the Broadway diagonal at the base, with the double height segmented curved mechanical barrel mediating the rotation between the two massings. The six story base was designed to integrate the Times Square signage requirements architectonically. The materials—aluminum, polished stainless steel, glass and mirror—produce a constantly changing graphic, from opacity to reflectivity, depending upon the natural light variation.

The building lobby, connecting 47th and 48th streets, is a horizontal space, defined by an integrated granite and marble floor and wall design, with a coffered wood ceiling.

Subsequent interior design extended to executive offices, dining, meeting spaces, and a boardroom on the 40th and 41st floors, to the main lobby at street level, and to a cafeteria on the lower level.

The corporate cafeteria, accessed from the lobby through a transparent double height vertical circulation space, added a new dimensional and volumetric interplay, transforming the basement into an environmentally sensitive and architecturally integrated spatial extension of the public realm.

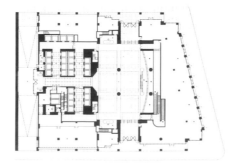

Cafeteria from lobby | Servery | Lower- and ground-level plans

Sony Entertainment Headquarters

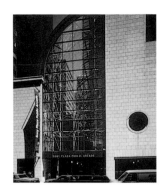

In 1993, Sony Corporation acquired the celebrated AT&T Building designed by Philip Johnson for their music entertainment division.

The program initiated the redesign and enclosure of the previously outdoor, sixty foot high arcades and public plaza at the building's base. The north and south arcades fronting Madison Avenue were transformed into retail spaces, with large scale electronic graphics and displays for the company's varied products.

The public plaza, connecting 55th and 56th streets, was redesigned as a new "urban landscaped square" connecting the new retail spaces, the building's lobby, and the existing two story "annex" building on the west side of the space. The annex was redesigned to accommodate a newsstand, store, commissary, cafe, ticket booth, and the Sony Wonder Museum, an interactive, state-of-the-art, electronic environment exhibiting communication technology.

The 1,000,000 square foot, thirty-five story tower was renovated to accommodate 1,600 employees, a significant increase from the original 600 housed by AT&T.

A rigorous architectural strategy, incorporating the original custom perforated metal ceilings and the building core was developed to accommodate the multiple entertainment divisions and identities. The integrated material palette, graphics and interior planning modules, afforded the required variations, flexibility and hierarchies within a unified structure.

The original white marble sky lobby, connecting the tower floors to the building lobby, was redesigned as the new reception/waiting space, and reimagined—through the addition of anegre wood paneling, black glass and Dorothea Rockbourne murals as a graphic counterpoint to the original architecture and initiating reference to the new corporate palette.

The renovation also included a 75 seat screening room, corporate cafeteria and store, executive dining and conference space, and a new restaurant suite at the top of the building, with panoramic views of Central Park and the city.

Atrium/public plaza   Atrium façade from south | Detail of public plaza | Retail space

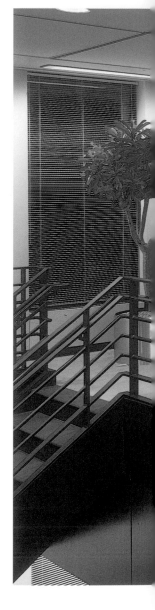

Typical circulation gallery | Executive office

Executive dining

PepsiCo World Headquarters

PURCHASE, NEW YORK

In 1993, Pepsi Co sought to reprogram and renovate selective portions of its World Headquarters, an interconnected, seven building, 400,000 square foot complex, originally designed by Edward Durrell Stone in a suburban park setting, with an extensive landscaping and sculpture gardens by Russell Page and Francois Goflinet.

The first phase accommodated a new 400 seat cafeteria, servery, and food preparation area on the lower level of the main entry pavilion. The second phase added a two story high glass dining pavilion extension connecting the cafeteria, as well as a new reception/gallery space with adjacent rooms, conference center, and boardroom.

Adjacent to the main entry pavilion, the new Leadership Conference Center, a state of the art meeting facility, was incorporated by excavating the entry floor level to accommodate the required stepped-seating and stage. The main meeting room accommodates 150 participants, with each seating component equipped with data ports, individual microphones, and speakers. Serving the meeting space are two thousand square feet of flexible, subdividable, acoustically isolated, breakout conference space.

The entire design reflects the interactive and multiparticipatory philosophy of PepsiCo.

Pavilion addition to existing Edward Durrell Stone building

Dining pavilion | Servery | Meeting room gallery

The Herbert Irving
Comprehensive Cancer Center

NEW YORK PRESBYTERIAN HOSPITAL   NEW YORK, NEW YORK

Two distinct but related facilities were designed for the five-story Herbert Irving Comprehensive Cancer Center—one for adult patients, the other for pediatric patients.

The Medical/Surgical Oncology Center includes radiology, gynecology and surgical departments, a day-hospital, examination rooms, consultation and procedure rooms, a pharmacy, laboratory, and patient counseling areas, as well as group, semi-private and private treatment areas and administrative space.

Patients enter through a light-filled elevator lobby—finished with glass wall panels, stone flooring, and a vaulted wood ceiling—into an open reception area. An arc shape in the ceiling, mirrored in the floor pattern and desk design, directs patients to smaller waiting areas to the north and south. These sub-waiting areas are centrally located between groups of examination and consultation rooms, and provide more privacy to patients and manageability for staff. The open group and semi-private chemotherapy areas are arranged to minimize visual clutter, facilitate staff efficiency, and take advantage of views, including the Hudson River.

The Pediatric Oncology Center is an outpatient examination, diagnostic, and treatment facility for children, from infancy to 18 years old. Extensive interviews with staff and discussions with former patients and family members helped generate a design that allows patients and caregivers to continue, as much as possible, their usual activities while at the hospital.

Reception, elevator lobby

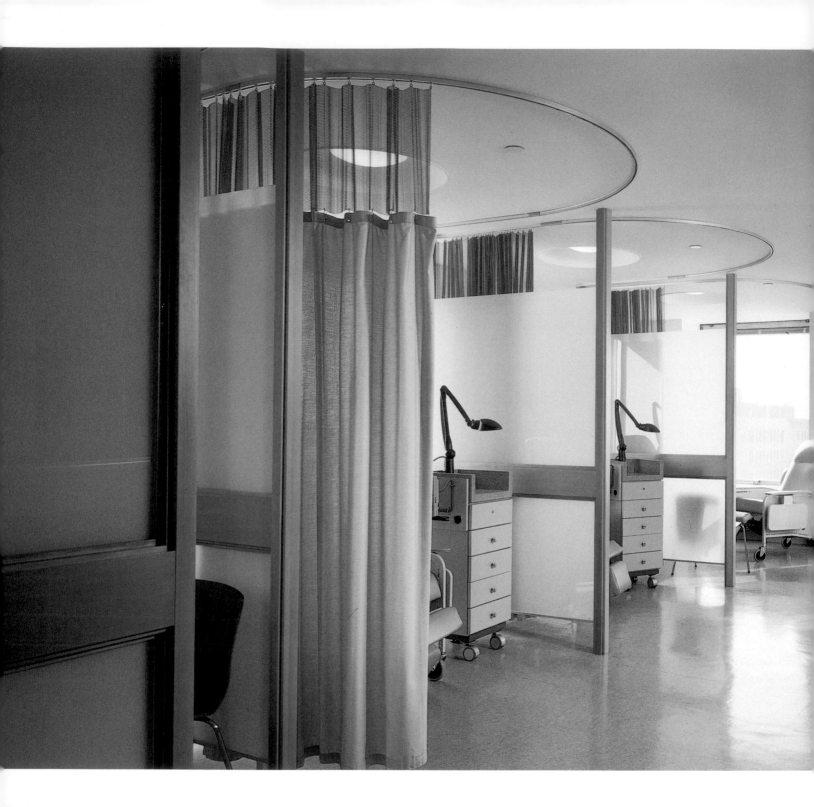

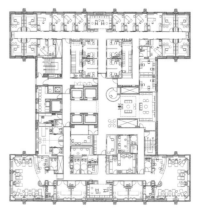

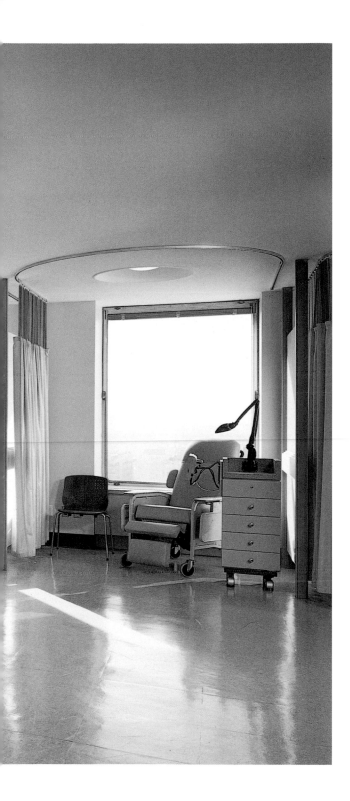

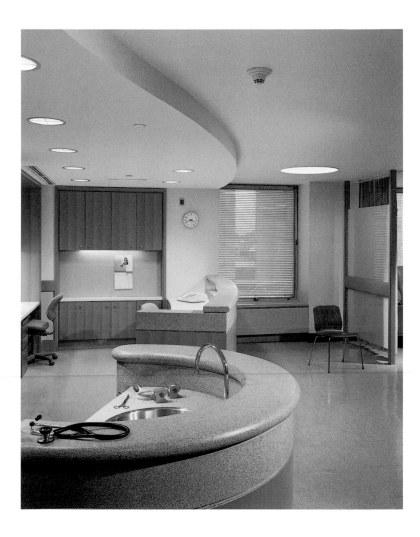

The elevator lobby, with its softly waving pale blue ceiling dotted with star-shaped lights of white glass, flows into the large main space that extends from one end of the floor to the other. It encompasses waiting and activity areas for all age groups and unifies these with exam, treatment and other patient support areas. A colorful full-height curvilinear wall on one side and the "Thick Wall" with patient lockers and toy storage on the other serve as visual landmarks throughout the floor. Within the open areas and adjacent to group treatment and exam rooms, a long curved banquette defines a quiet activity area. A low divider, made from oversized "blocks," separates an area just for toddlers. Teenagers can find more independent haven in a semi-circular, den-like lounge. A family lounge overlooking the Hudson River provides eating facilities, while a parents' lounge (a "kid-free" zone) affords adults a place to take an emotional break, do research, talk with other parents, or work.

The entire space was designed as an integrated graphic and architectural experience, transforming the normative into an unexpected, visually stimulating and engaging environment for both the patients and parents.

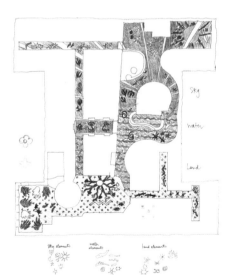

The Lauder Foundation

NEW YORK, NEW YORK

Seven years after the completion of his corporate offices, Ronald S. Lauder took similar space in the same Manhattan tower for his prominent philanthropic enterprises. This provided an opportunity, not simply to replicate the original offices, but to revisit and reinterpret the space.

The Austrian Secessionist furniture and art collection were integrated to the design, enriching the spatial articulation as well as reinforcing the craft ethic and materiality of the space.

The rhythmic plan of offices and the graphically articulated axial circulation gallery are transformed by the modular ceiling sequence of perforated stainless steel barrel vaults, running the length of the space.

The integrated cherry millwork and custom designed work stations, combined with the two color rubber tile floor and asymmetrical glass block inset strip in the gallery, establish a sense of quality and density consistent with the Foundation's intellectual and visionary philosophy.

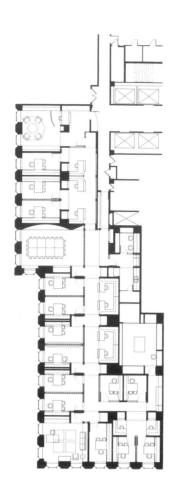

Plan | Private offices | Conference room

Detail of circulation gallery

Pace Wildenstein Gallery

BEVERLY HILLS, CALIFORNIA

The Pace-Wildenstein galleries occupy parts of three separate buildings at the intersection of Wilshire Boulevard and Rodeo Drive. The entrance, off a narrow alley into the first building, was enlarged and cut away to establish a more visible entry presence.

The reception area mediates the change in level between the entrance and the ground floor exhibition space in the second building, where a 17-foot high ceiling accommodates large sculptures and paintings by contemporary artists. The walls of this gallery are rotated slightly from the orthogonal column grid, maximizing uninterrupted wall surfaces, and creating a new pure volume within a space whose perimeter had been compromised by columns, ducts, and pipes.

A wide stair leads to a mezzanine, lit by six new windows, overlooking the main floor. The stair continues from the mezzanine to another gallery on the second floor of the third building. Here, the grid of the existing columns and beams is used to modulate the long interior volume along Rodeo Drive, creating a series of intimate galleries, suitable for exhibiting smaller works, drawings and photographs.

Along the perimeter of the building, a "floating" wall, articulated by a single row of glass block at either end, stops at the underside of the beams, and is lit from behind. In addition to controlling natural light from five existing windows, the wall creates both the primary hanging surface and a "street façade" for the gallery. Behind and beyond the exhibition area are private offices and viewing rooms, accessible from both the gallery space and a separate elevator lobby.

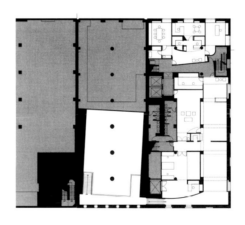

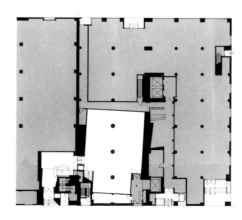

Office reception

Ian Schrager Corporate Offices

NEW YORK, NEW YORK

The design of this 15,000 square foot industrial loft space expresses the minimal, yet visionary philosophy of this design oriented company.

The articulation of "space as frame," exposing the existing concrete structure as the primary reference, is reinforced by the concept of transparency, integrated work stations, cabinet work, and files, all "floating" below an eight foot high transom datum, that also houses the ambient uplighting throughout.

The interior landscape of white-painted, high and low partition walls creates a series of compressed and expanded spaces; i.e., public and circulation spaces are compressed and culminate in expansive exterior views or large interior spaces.

The transparent perimeter executive offices, open work stations and support space within a natural and indirect light filled, white, architecturally integrated environment, establishes appropriate setting for objects and creative intervention.

Arriving at the orange elevator lobby and passing through the frosted glass entry door heightens the sense of lightness, whiteness and surreal calm.

President's office

168   View from southwest

The David Geffen Foundation Building

This 90,000 square foot corporate headquarters is located in the Beverly Hills industrial district. Though zoning restrictions limit the height of buildings to three stories, site and program variants provoked a complex, asymmetrically articulated building. A cylindrical, translucent skylight, running the length of the building and incorporating the third-floor executive offices, reinterprets the form of the traditional cornice along the street, and establishes a unifying and iconic silhouette.

The main entrance is a distinct volume created by the extension of the cylinder carving into the facade. From inside, this form is understood again—as the skylight "cornice" becomes both roof and window wall on the third floor, challenging conventional expectations of corporate office space.

The orchestration of exterior and interior forms and volumes is critical to the design. At the southeast corner, a rotated tower terminates the ramped arcade from the main entrance and redefines the adjoining pedestrian plaza; inside, the skylit tower houses two graduated stacked conference rooms. The film-screening room on the second floor, is articulated as a separate volume, projecting towards the street at the southwest corner, creating a canopy over the garage entry and paralleling the ramp, forming the required sloped floor. The three story, conical, skylite public atrium is the central interior volume, anchoring the core and establishing a referential, orientation form/volume on each floor.

Zinc and Kalwall express the contrapuntal materiality of the objects from the limestone and granite primary frame of the building, transforming the typical to a site specific collage.

Detail of south facade and entry | Detail of south facade and entry

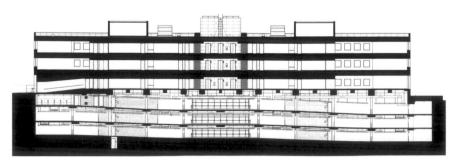

Detail of atrium | Atrium/reception | Longitudinal section

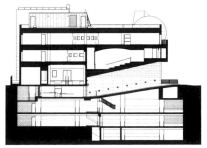

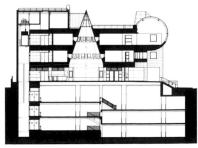

Kalwall and glass office space at third-level | Cross section through screening room and garage ramp | Cross section through atrium and office space

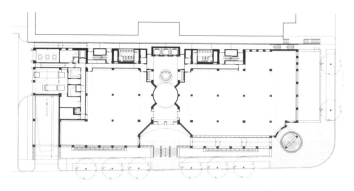

Detail of tower skylight | Detail of tower and fountain toward ramp arcade | View from southeast

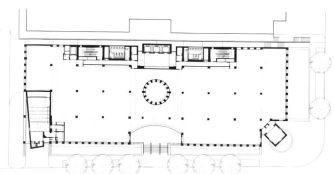

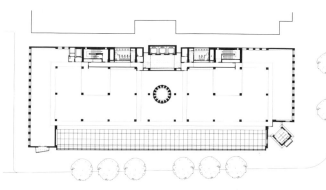

Ground-, second- and third-level plans   173

Maple Associates Ltd.

BEVERLY HILLS, CALIFORNIA

This four story, 160,000 square foot office building, with a three level, 466 car below grade parking structure is located in the Beverly Hills industrial area, two blocks north of the Geffen Foundation Building.

Designed on a midblock, street fronting site, the parabolic segmented courtyard with its surrounding covered arcades extends the landscaped entry sequence, from the sidewalk, through the fountain/reflecting pool front yard, under the open east/west bridge connecting the two wings, to the two story entry lobby.

The sequence is reinforced by a grid of sixteen ficus trees, initiated at the sidewalk and continuing as an allée through the courtyard, which is the central referential space in the building.

The massing presents a multi-scaled composite building, that is site specific and context sensitive, while simultaneously affording unique planning and tenant flexibility.

The materials—grey-green granite, glass, zinc and aluminum panels—further articulate the hierarchical massing, extending the formal object/frame strategy of the Geffen Foundation Building.

View from southeast

View from northwest | Courtyard | View from street

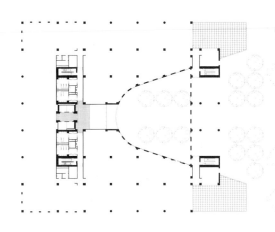

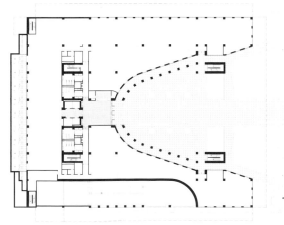

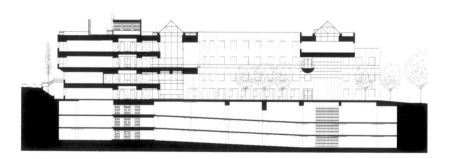

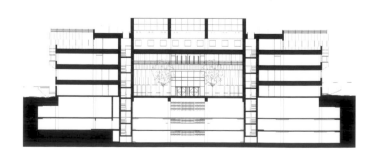

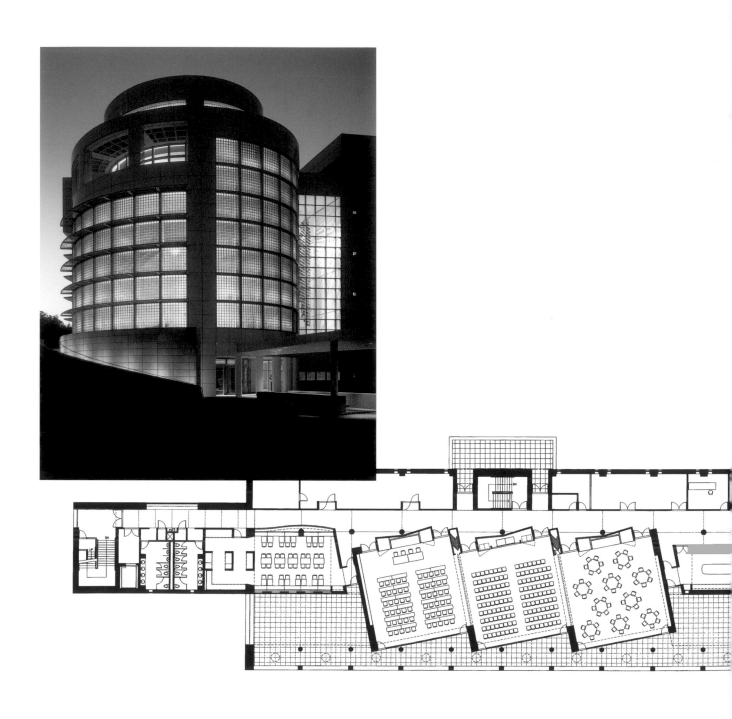

Cultural & Institutional

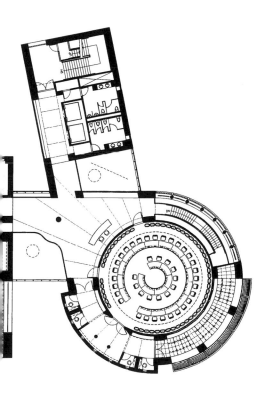

East Academic Complex
Eugenio Maria de Hostos
Community College

THE CITY UNIVERSITY OF NEW YORK   BRONX, NEW YORK

This multi-purpose building for a community college in a Spanish-speaking area of the Bronx represents a composite program in a dense urban context. The building provides classrooms, faculty and student offices, a swimming pool, gymnasium and ancillary athletic spaces, a 1000-seat proscenium theater, a 350-seat repertory theater, faculty and student dining facilities, a campus store, an art gallery and studios, and a pedestrian bridge over the Grand Concourse, linking the existing campus buildings to the new structure.

The building contains many departments with diverse and varied functions, organized and unified around a five-story skylit atrium. Articulated horizontally with balconies and vertically with stairs, the atrium is both the major public space on campus and the primary circulation volume.

Although site and budget constraints were severe, the program offered an opportunity to create architecture with a significant presence. The Grand Concourse façade reinforces the built edge, establishes a gateway to the college, and together with the original campus structure, defines an outdoor courtyard. The tower and bridge serve as visual icons in the community, establishing a sense of place and a new image for the college.

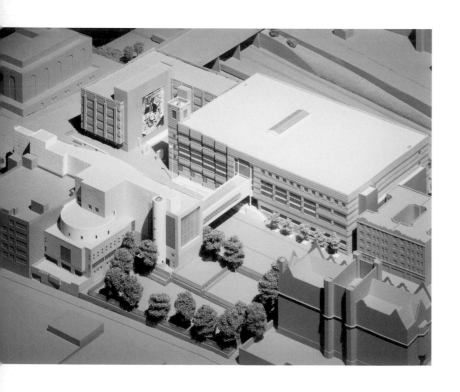

Grand Concourse, bridge, and east academic building

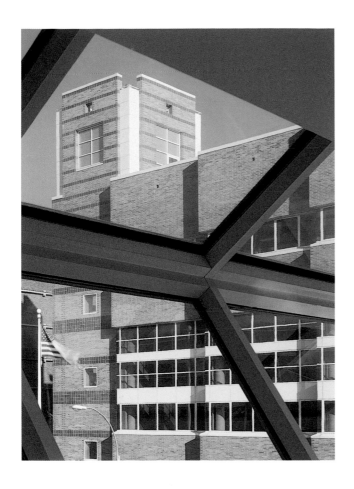

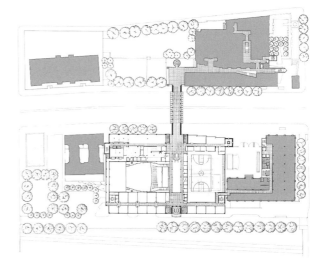

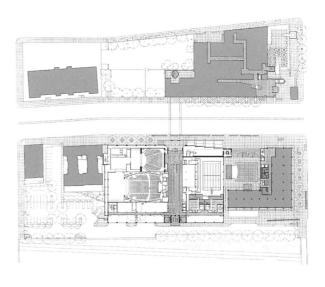

Pedestrian bridge
Tower from pedestrian bridge | Detail of bridge and tower | Bridge- and ground-level plans

Social Sciences Building and Super Computer Center

UNIVERSITY OF CALIFORNIA SAN DIEGO   LA JOLLA, CALIFORNIA

Set between Southern California's mountains and coastline, this building was a two-phase project completed over a four-year period. It was an opportunity to add to the structural presence of the campus, and also redefine its primary pedestrian circulation spine.

The first phase of development, the Social Sciences Building, is sited adjacent to Campus Walk, reinforcing its north-south axis. A series of wings, containing faculty and student offices, perpendicular and rotated off the east side of this linear building, create a set of sloped grass courtyards. Large open portals at the base of the building provide views through the structure to the mountains and establish a sense of porosity between Campus Walk and the major outdoor green spaces. Each courtyard is at once unique and referential to the circulation spine.

The second phase, a faculty office building and a new super computer laboratory, anchors the entire assemblage. A pre-existing computer building was renovated into office space and given a façade consistent with the new complex, creating a fourth distinct courtyard. The new element, parallel to the center wing of the Social Sciences Building, reaches toward Campus Walk.

The north façade of the Super Computer Center is an iconic gateway to and from Campus Walk. Its tilted window panels are unique to the complex and provide faculty with views of the ocean. The use of cross-ventilation to take advantage of the ocean breezes was an integral design consideration, making air-conditioning unnecessary. Every office has operable jalousie windows, a fan, and transoms over the doors.

The black tile tower contains three levels of computer training rooms, which purposely have no natural light. The tile, which reads as two-dimensional trim when used around the bay window frames, here is utilized to articulate a three-dimensional volume. The tower becomes an object in the courtyard—a symbolic, sculptural building. Its roof is an open terrace with ocean and mountain views.

The materiality creates a building that appears both carved from a solid and, at the same time, highly articulated and responsive to environmental considerations.

View from southwest campus walk | View from northwest

Ground level arcade and terraces

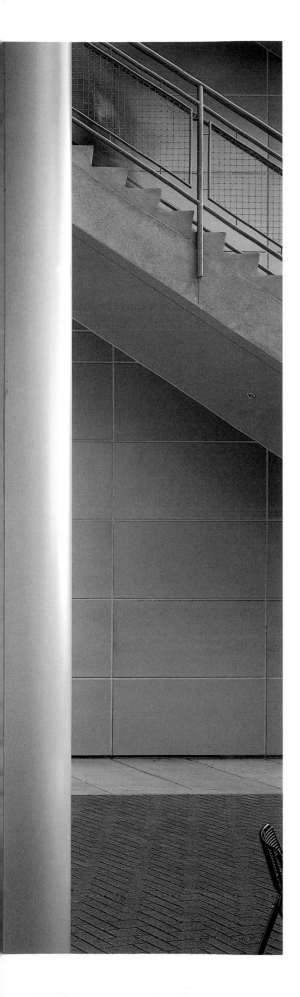

Department Of Political Science

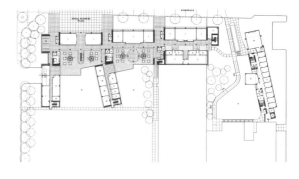

Detail of west façade | Detail of stair

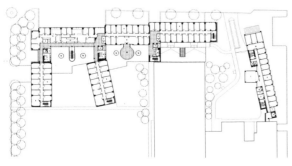

Healy Hall toward entry bridge and circulation library

The Science, Industry and Business Library

THE NEW YORK PUBLIC LIBRARY   NEW YORK, NEW YORK

SIBL is the New York Public Library's largest undertaking since the construction of the main building at Fifth Avenue and 42nd Street in 1911. Filling seven floors of the landmarked B. Altman Building, this intervention transforms the midtown Manhattan department store, designed by Trowbridge & Livingston, into an interactive resource for the information age, retaining the building exterior's classical integrity while incorporating advanced computer technologies into the infrastructure.

SIBL's large windows invite Madison Avenue pedestrians to look into one of the few monumental interior public spaces in New York City with an immediate street-level impact: a two-story atrium created by removing a major portion of the existing first floor. This significant and strategic reconfiguration of usable space transforms the typical preconception of basement, creating a 44,000-square-foot public reading space that, with the exception of the circulating library on the new bridge level, consolidates all of the primary reference and staff facilities on one level.

The renovated facility reinforces SIBL's image as a "library without borders," a transparent membrane through which information and resources freely shift between the library, various business and research communities, and the public. SIBL accommodates an open-shelf reference collection, periodical shelving, catalog areas, reference specialists supported by a complete reference department, open microfilm shelving, reading areas, an electronic information center, a training center, 60,000 square feet of remote storage stacks to hold 1.5 million volumes, and a full-service circulation library with 60,000 volumes, various assembly spaces and 50,000 square feet of administrative offices.

In view of accommodating new information technologies as they emerge, flexibility and accessibility were integral to the design. One hundred computerized workstations in the Electronic Information Center provide free public access to the Internet and other electronic research tools, and five hundred stations in the Research and Circulating libraries are set up to accommodate patrons' laptop computers. The unpredictability of equipment sizes made standard library dimensions inadequate. Instead, workstations are separated by adaptable perforated dividers that offer lateral flexibility, create a definable territory, and are handicapped-accessible.

Entry from Madison Avenue

Entry hall from information desk

Healy Hall from lower-level circulation space

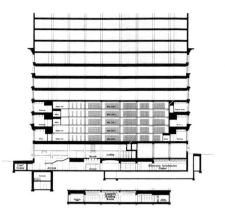

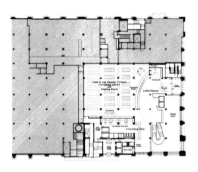

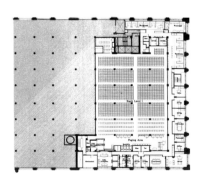

Excellent sight lines allow the entire Research Library to be supervised by relatively few people, freeing the librarians from "security duty" and allowing them to do specialized research or to consult with individual readers in small conference rooms.

SIBL staff areas surround the stacks on the second through fourth floors. The three uppermost levels are used for general New York Public Library administration.

A genuinely hybrid institution, SIBL was designed to merge the familiarity of books with the initially intimidating abstractions of networks and databases. The combination of traditional (stone, wood) and contemporary (stainless steel, terrazzo) materials illustrates both the humanist roots of the library-as-institution and its ability to adapt to change.

Lower-level research reading area | Lower-level information center

Lower-level research library circulation desk from Healy Hall

View from reflecting pool/plaza

Museum of Contemporary Art

NORTH MIAMI, FLORIDA

The creation of a contemporary art museum in a mixed commercial and residential pocket of North Miami transformed a public parking lot into an animated destination point and redefined the downtown area as a cultural center.

Part of an urban revitalization project, this publicly funded museum mediates between City Hall and Police Headquarters, providing pedestrian circulation to every part of the trio of civic buildings. MOCA defines a new public plaza, prefaced by a grid of palm trees, a large reflecting pool, and a versatile pavilion used for concerts and other performances, films, installations, and art education programs.

Four articulated and interconnected "elements," rendered in colored stucco, glass block, with galvanized corrugated-metal roofs, combine to form an intense visual collage that invites visitors to engage with both the art and architecture. The emphasis on community interaction evinced by the generous public space continues within the museum, which by its accessibility and rendering, suggests that art is meant to be experienced, used, and incorporated into one's life—rather than mutely and passively observed.

Such approachability is crucial for a museum determined to fuse community outreach and the recognition of regional artists with international art on the cutting edge.

The structures frame an exterior courtyard accessed from the lobby, which was designed as an exhibition space along with the main gallery, a totally flexible and reconfigurable space that accommodates a multiplicity of exhibition venues.

The overall site/building/landscape strategy established a new, relevant and memorable sense of place.

Aerial view from north

Entry arcade

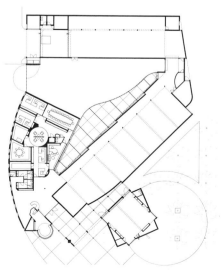

Levitt Center for University Advancement

UNIVERSITY OF IOWA   IOWA CITY, IOWA

Visible form many parts of the city, particularly at night, the Levitt Center, clad in white metal panels, glass block, and Indiana limestone, is an asymmetrical assemblage of geometric forms that articulate a hierarchical sequence of public gathering spaces and private work areas.

The building is an inversion of the typical configuration of public spaces on the ground level with offices above. Here office floors act as a pedestal for major public spaces that overview the campus, river, and park. The five-story rotunda, the exterior of which marks a visual and lateral edge of the university's Performing Arts Campus, anchors the complex and acts as its main public meeting and circulation space.

The three-story interior of the rotunda is a "vertical lobby" encircled by a ceremonial stair and cantilevered bridges that create a promenade, leading visitors to the assembly spaces at the top of the building. This atrium space integrates numerous works of art by faculty, students, and local artists.

The top floor of the building's bar element contains three "peaks"-double-height assembly halls that are rotated to provide views of the river. The rotation creates a series of connected but distinct solids, and a series of discrete areas on the roof terrace. The three rooms can be combined into one, seating approximately 1,000, or can be divided and used simultaneously for different functions such as receptions, lectures, or dinners. The sculptural forms of these rooms distinguish their public functions from the three floors of administrative offices below and define a "cornice" to the arts campus.

A double height, circular boardroom "caps" the rotunda. This flexible space, with an inverted dome ceiling, features sophisticated audio/video equipment and concentric, cherry and stone conference tables. A portion of the rotunda is carved to create a private covered terrace with views of the river and theater.

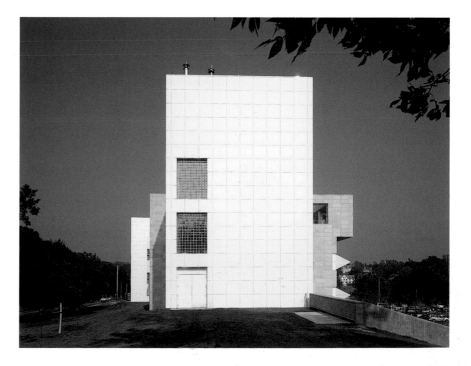

Detail of rotunda and lower-level entry

View from southeast across Iowa River | West façade

Rotunda | Main entry | Rotunda stair   Detail of rotunda

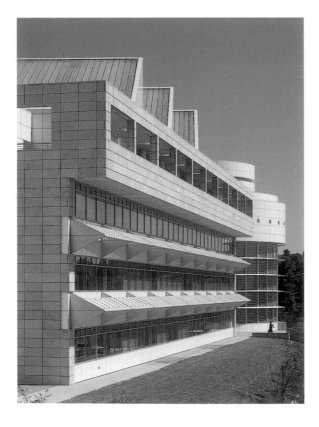

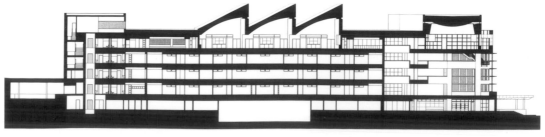

Flexible multi-use meeting/lecture rooms | View from southwest | Longitudinal section

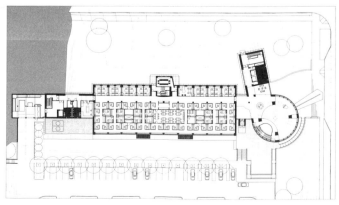

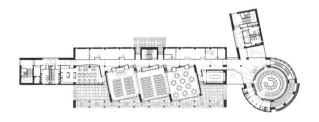

Roof terrace | Boardroom | Roof terrace   Boardroom roof terrace

Henry Art Gallery
Renovation and Addition

UNIVERSITY OF WASHINGTON   SEATTLE, WASHINGTON

The original Henry Art Gallery, a 10,000 square foot, two-story masonry structure designed by Carl F. Gould in 1927, was overshadowed by large neighboring buildings and compromised by a necessary but poorly conceived pedestrian bridge. The new main gallery separates the museum and addition from adjacent structures, affording a significant sense of place and architectural identity, and reroutes the entry sequence and transition from community to campus, completing the museum complex within its contextual frame. The intervention unifies disparate elements in both contrapuntal and asymmetrical variations, horizontally and vertically, experienced as forms, from the exterior and re-experienced as spaces from within.

The addition is an architectural collage that introduces new structures and new materials and carves away at existing ones, revealing fragments and interactions. The three-story addition—a linear structure of textured stainless steel, cast-in-place concrete and cast stone—offsets the dense original building. It houses versatile top-lighted galleries, administrative offices, storage and conservation facilities, as well as a new lobby, lecture theater and museum store.

The pedestrian bridge is reoriented to be on axis with the Suzzalo Library entry at the heart of the campus. At the existing building entry, the site was excavated to create a sunken outdoor sculpture court. This excavation allowed the original first floor to function as a piano nobile and the lower level to be re-perceived as a space at grade rather than as a basement.

To ease pedestrian site penetration, and to preserve axial views from Campus Parkway to Suzzalo Library as well as the statue of George Washington, a portion of the linear structure is "compressed" below grade. This compression leaves fragments or traces in the form of three lanterns, which articulate the gatelike porosity of the site and bring natural light to the administrative offices. The remainder of the building pushes forward to the street under a curved, skylighted roof—a "foothill" to the campus.

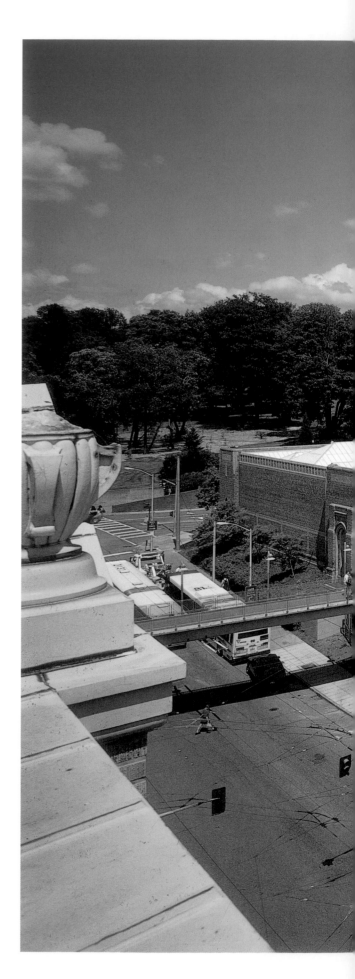

View from 15th Street

View of original building and addition from 15th Street | View east from pedestrian bridge

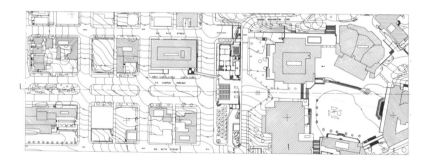

As one descends into the main gallery—a space that has been previewed from the top-most landing of the stair—there is an inversion of expectation: rather than becoming smaller and darker, the building becomes more spacious and light-filled. At each level, visitors become aware of the connection between the existing and the new spaces. The juxtaposition of historical and contemporary imagery is revealed through the counter-point between the permanent collection and special exhibits as well as through the passage from the renovated building into the new structure. In the main gallery, visitors see the original Henry façade through a window at the sculpture terrace level, and are thus re-oriented to the overall context.

Plaza from north toward new entry

East façade from campus | Detail of entry | Entry ramp toward original building   New main stair

Richard Long
Puget Sound Mud Cir
April 11 – August 31

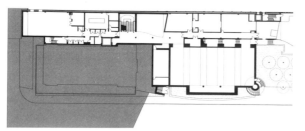

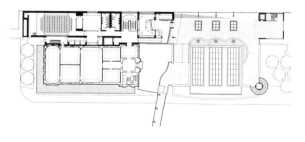

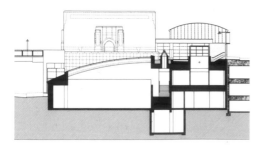

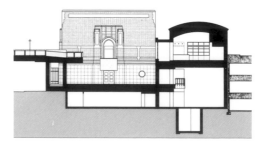

Main gallery stair | Main gallery stair from lower-level stair landing | Main gallery and stair from middle level | Sections

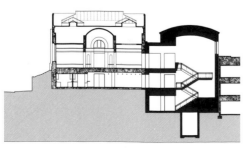

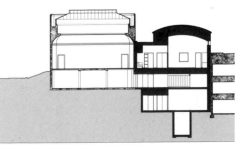

The luminous cylindrical shaft at the core of the exterior spiral stair anchors the southwest corner of the main gallery and the site. As fragments, the exterior forms of the building imply but do not directly reveal their spaces; anticipation, sequential revelation, and memory are as crucial to the experience of the complex as the physical manifestation.

Detail of main gallery | View of spiral stair "column"

James S. McDonnell Hall

PRINCETON UNIVERSITY   PRINCETON, NEW JERSEY

Princeton's new undergraduate physics building forms a visual and physical link between the existing Jadwin and Fine Halls, greatly expanding teaching facilities, resolving incompatible building scales and site complexities, and creating a math and physics cluster. The new building also defines the intersection of the primary automobile approach to campus and a major cross-campus pedestrian axis.

Three major programmatic components—lecture halls, classrooms, and teaching laboratories—are articulated as discrete elements in their massing and materiality. Compressed partially below grade, two teaching theaters form a brick "base" for two building "objects." A cast-stone volume, housing classrooms and service areas, transforms the existing plaza into a more defined courtyard. A zinc-clad element housing labs and flexible teaching spaces is rotated to resolve the different geometries of the two adjacent buildings. The barrel-vaulted roof over the labs, visible from the taller adjacent buildings, is treated as a fifth façade.

A double-height canopy fronting College Walk, marks the main entrance to the building. The entrance at grade serves the labs and classrooms on levels one and two. An exterior stair leads down to a second entrance that allows students going to lectures to quietly bypass the classroom areas, and the public to access the lecture halls and library after hours. This entrance serves a 6,000 square foot gallery below the plaza that serves as a connection between the existing buildings, and as a lobby area for the two new lecture halls, capable of accommodating up to 1,000 students during class changeovers.

The new lecture halls incorporate unique features that support Princeton's method of teaching undergraduate physics, yet remain flexible enough to accommodate other university functions. Concealed catwalks, thirty feet above the stage, are used to launch, drop, and swing objects to demonstrate natural phenomena. Twenty-four-foot-diameter turntables are inset into each stage, allowing experiments, some of which take several days to set up, to be rotated back-of-the-house while other presentations are being made.

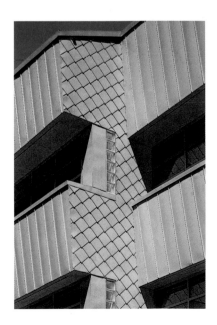

The building's exterior palette was chosen to engage in a dialogue with the Jadwyn/Fine complex and the Venturi laboratory across Washington Road. The striped pattern restates the bold graphics of the Venturi building while picking up the scale and texture of Jadwin's brick. The taupe cast-stone of the classroom "block" reinforces the color and texture of Fine Tower. The most visible part of the building is sheathed in standing-seam zinc panels and zinc shingles. The zinc used on the exterior walls is carried up onto the roof, further articulating the iconic lab element.

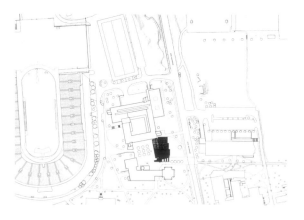

View from College Walk | Lecture theater stairs from College Walk | Site plan

Renovated lecture theater lobby | Turntable stage

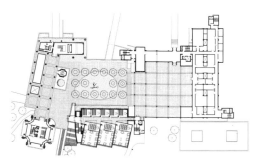

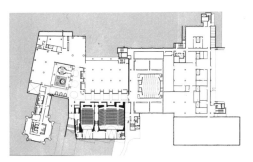

Laboratory gallery | Laboratory classroom Stair from landing

Institute for Human Performance, Rehabilitation and Biomedical Research

STATE UNIVERSITY OF NEW YORK AT SYRACUSE   SYRACUSE, NEW YORK

This four-story facility for education, research, and patient care incorporates a 19,000 square foot gymnasium, a 75-foot medical therapy swimming pool, a full-service orthopedic treatment center, and a 100 flexible, state-of-the-art.

The design evolved from precise and extensive technical criteria and provides climate-controlled space for multiple medical and recreational functions. Public and private domains are expressed by the solid/void relationships and the penetration of light.

The building is composed of three, parallel, two-story laboratory wings, and joined by two skylit interior courtyards. The wings house research units designed for maximum efficiency and flexibility in mechanical and utility configurations. The south, four story atrium houses the main entrance, circulation and multi-use public space at ground level.

The north, three story atrium forms the central volume of the gymnasium which accommodates a track, playing courts and extensive exercise equipment, over the medical examination treatment center, accessed from the south atrium.

Both atriums afford views to the spaces below as well as across to opposite wings, enhancing the sense of a communal, collegial environment.

The composite program and varying functions, as well as the the urban context, impacted the design parti and clarified the volumetric and massing organization articulated by a material palette of two bricks, stainless steel and glass.

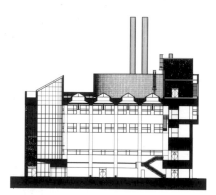

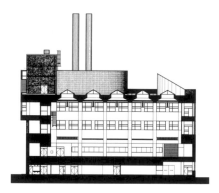

View from northwest

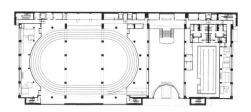 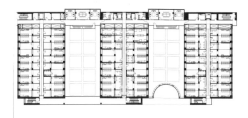

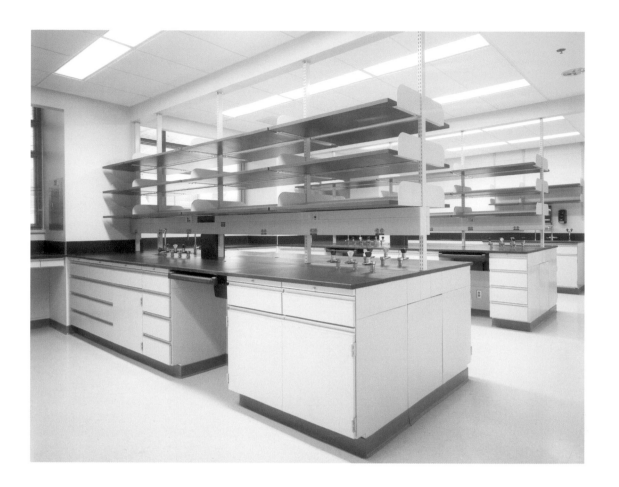

Typical lab module | Research therapy swimming pool

Nanyang Polytechnic

ANG MO KIO, SINGAPORE

Conceived of as a pedestrian-oriented urban village, Nanyang Polytechnic is an interactive educational community. Modeled on the University of Virginia, in the sense that there is a main iconic building, the campus extends to the north and south from the central multi-use atrium that houses common facilities.

The Administration/Student Center/Library building orients itself east and west to the major courtyards that are articulated by the lecture theater spaces in each college. Despite its size (the Administrative building alone is 500,000 square feet), the integration of courtyards and outdoor spaces, and the modulation of façades that define them, offer a variety and scale breakdown that makes the campus read more like a village than a mega-structure.

Because it combines functions that are often designed as separate entities, the multi-use Campus Center/Atrium is at once economical, practical, and communal, a space that engenders dialogue between disciplines. Its complexity of program, strategic location, and spectacular presence make it an iconic destination place.

One enters on a lower level in a retail/student services/office arcade after passing a major reflecting pond on axis with the building. The scale of the entry space is monumental, establishing a critical mass and representing the importance of the institution. From this space, one can ascend escalators to pedestrian bridges, circulate through to the courtyard that accesses the student food court, or access the main theater.

A system of cloisters and covered walkways provides access to the four schools (Engineering, Health Sciences, Business Management, and Information Technology) as well as to all administrative and common-use facilities. The circulation system integrates covered outdoor terraces and is designed to form a series of landscaped outdoor spaces, gardens, and courtyards that offer a multiplicity of visual references and a sense of orientation.

The daily process of arrival, circulation, and return provides a sequence of varied visual and functional experiences. The organization of the campus integrates architecture, outdoor space, and pedestrian circulation systems in a way that is psychologically uplifting and inspirational. Circulation is conceived of as a circular loop system with no dead ends. Multiple options are available, but the primary route from the main entrance to all facilities is direct and logical.

　　Campus site model | Graded site before construction

Main entry courtyard arcade and Campus Center

Main entry courtyard/arcade and Campus Center | Vehicular circulation diagram | Pedestrian circulation diagram | Colleges and courtyards diagram

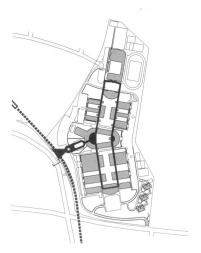
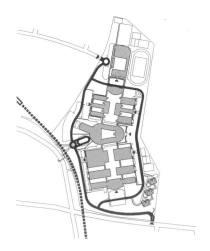
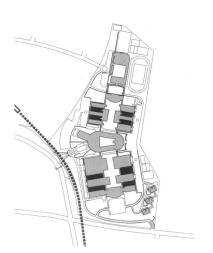

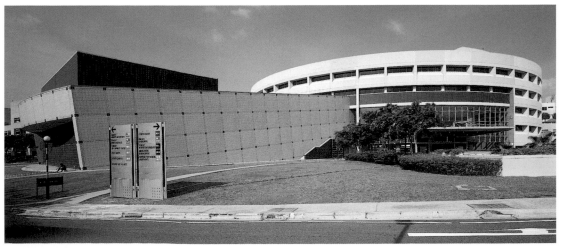

Campus Center atrium

Detail of pedestrian bridges in Campus Center atrium

Campus Center atrium

South garden | Courtyard façade detail

North courtyard

View from south | Tent covered amphitheater

Engineering laboratory | Engineering classroom

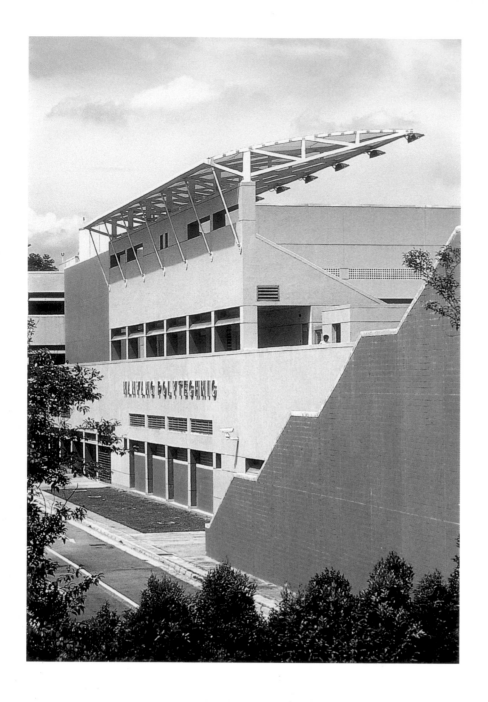

Stadium entrance | Track and field stadium

University Technology and Learning Complex

LAWRENCE TECHNOLOGICAL UNIVERSITY
SOUTHFIELD, MICHIGAN

This project afforded the opportunity to initiate a new campus master plan and build the critical first phase, transforming both the physical and psychological presence of the university.

The four-story, 435 foot long, 135,000 square foot, structure connects the existing Architecture and Engineering School buildings, presenting a new image to the campus. The integral three story covered portal is both the center's entry and the campus gateway, accessing the new central quadrangle, redesigned from a vehicular to a referential pedestrian outdoor space.

The four floor, north facing circulation/exhibition gallery affords continuous views of the quadrangle and accesses studio/classrooms on the south side's upper three floors, as well as a lecture theatre and seminar rooms. The ground level accommodates a reception space, a virtual reality laboratory, a two story exhibit hall, offices, and interconnection to the existing buildings. The lower level accommodates a TV studio and laboratories.

The exposed structure and mechanical systems, the integrated glazed south wall, sunscreens, and white interiors, foster the sense of openness and clarity in a learning, technology, research building.

The material palette of corrugated aluminum, white ceramic tile, and zinc shingles form a vibrant counterpoint to the existing masonry structures on the campus, implying both new aspirations and technological advancement in a revived university.

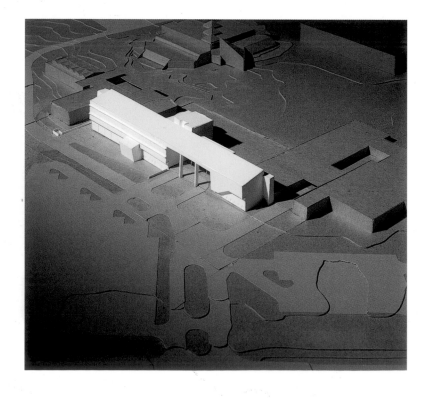

Site model

View from southeast toward entry court

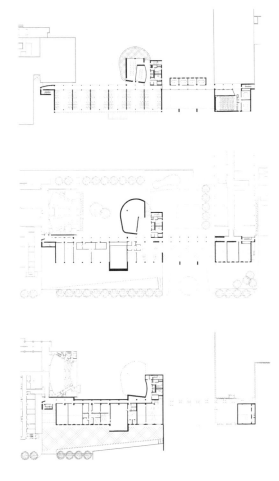

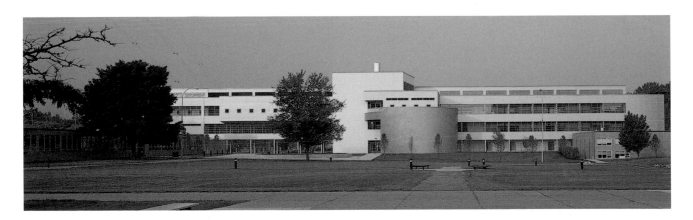

Detail of south façade toward lower-level courtyard   Detail of south façade | Fourth-, second, and lower-level plans | North façade from quad | South façade from street

Entry court

View of main entry below bridge | Detail of north façade

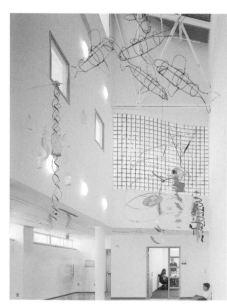

Detail of north façade | Lecture theater | Lecture theater lounge

Typical studio circulation gallery | Typical studio | Exhibition gallery

Main lobby and information kiosk

The Graduate Center

The Graduate Center houses the graduate school campus on twelve levels of neo-classical landmark B. Altman's Department Store Building. It includes the restoration of selected historic interior building elements, significant structural modifications to accommodate long-span spaces, and a complete technological infrastructure and environmental upgrade.

Public areas include: an auditorium, recital hall, black box theater/ screening room, TV studio, art gallery, bookstore/coffee bar, and conference center located on the ground and lower levels.

The academic and research areas, located on the middle five floors, include classrooms, lecture halls, computer labs, offices, and study areas. The top floors house administrative offices, a board room, and a conference center, organized around the central dining facility with views of the Empire State Building through a reconstructed major roof skylight.

The academic heart of the campus is the research library which occupies the entire second floor and portions of the ground and lower levels. It has its own internal vertical circulation system and a separate entrance from the main lobby.

Library facilities include open shelving for over 250,000 periodicals and monographs, 1,000 work stations of which more than half are wired to support either lap-top or desk-top computers, fully equipped state of the art Electronic Training Rooms, group study areas, miscellaneous special collection rooms, dissertation archives and music listening stations—all supporting the diverse and highly specialized academic departments.

The multiplicity of functions housed within the existing loft frame was our largest, most complex and composite renovation to date.

Elevator lobby | Martin E. Segal Theatre Center

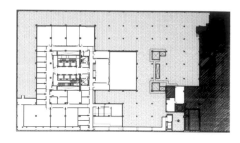

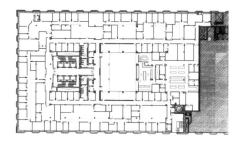

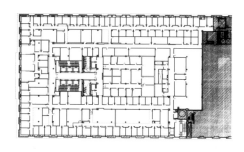

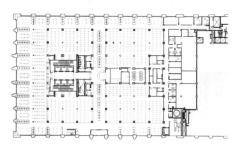

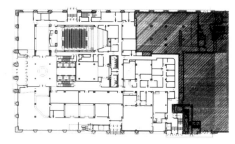

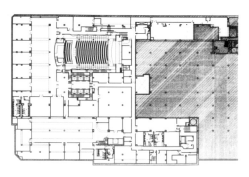

Ninth-, eighth-, third-, second-, ground-, and concourse-level plans | Library reader workstations | Computer classrooms | Research carrols   Library service desk

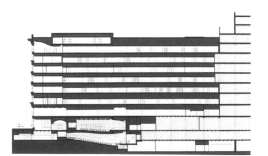

Conference room

Dining commons

International Center of Photography

NEW YORK, NEW YORK

The renovation of a 24,000 square foot ground- and lower-level space in an existing midtown Manhattan office building into a photography museum provided the opportunity to design a primary architectural environment for flexible and varying exhibition venues in a state-of-the-art environment.

The transparent street level entry accommodates a lobby reception space and museum store, as well as a series of flexible galleries which lead the viewer to the stair, seen from the lobby, which assesses the lower level galleries and cafe.

The anticipated descent is enhanced by this double height space—the referential volume in the gallery sequence. The space is articulated by the elevator core, the single stainless steel column, the stair and the iconic "cloud skylight" in the upper ceiling anchoring the memory.

The primary space of the museum was formed as an "excavation," resulting in an architecture that is sculptural, articulate, and primary, animated and enriched by the intervention of moveable walls and photographs, establishing a memorable collage of two creative disciplines.

Entry and lower level galleries from stair

View from stair toward lower-level galleries

Lower-level galleries | Ground- and lower-level plans

FSU Library for Information, Technology and Education

FERRIS STATE UNIVERSITY   BIG RAPIDS, MICHIGAN

FLITE is a 175,000 square foot complex that combines a traditional print library and state-of-the-art digital information library with a technological learning center. The building has been designed to provided a new architectural and symbolic presence to a campus of undistinguished post war buildings.

The siting of the building at the end of the primary town access road establishes a new campus entry, reconstituting a central campus parking lot into a major pedestrian quadrangle, and rerouting the vehicular circulation to the perimeter. The campus is transformed by a new iconic architecture, landscape and circulation system.

In addition to the library, FLITE houses an Educational Technology Center that includes an Instructional Technology Unit; a Center for Teaching, Learning and Faculty Department; and a Center for Distributed Learning. The design facilitates personal assistance with information needs and helps with finding, accessing, and utilizing expanded resources.

The 440,000-volume print collection of monographs, periodicals and documents is housed in standard open and compact shelving. It is interspersed with computer facilities and electronically equipped study, teaching and meeting rooms, allowing external electronic access.

The three main two story high "reading rooms," each programatically and architecturally unique, occur at the ground, second, and third levels, affording optimal research and study environments, as well as establishing a varied architectural and volumetric presence within the design.

The massing articulation and different façade scales address both orientation and specific site/campus contexts, allowing the building to be experienced as a multi-faceted object as well as a primary referential frame that combines and reverses the typical object/frame strategy of other projects.

Similar in principle to Lawrence Technological University, a single building initiated a new campus master plan, establishing a new iconic portal and an enriched sense of place.

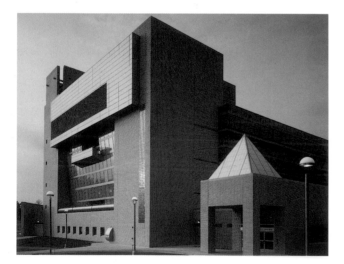

Detail of west entry pavilion | View from southwest | View from northwest from campus entry   Quad entry

Twenty-four hour study court

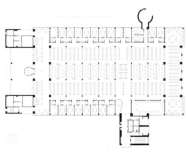

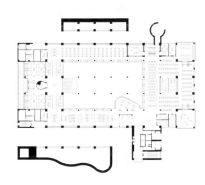

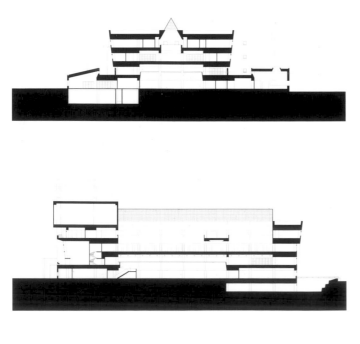

West atrium reading room | Cross section | Longitudinal section | Detail of spiral staircase

Upper atrium reading room and offices | Reference reading room | Periodical reading room and stacks | Reference stack workstation | Southeast view from quad (overleaf)

East façade from I-91

Naismith Memorial Basketball Hall of Fame

The building, viewed from both the Interstate Highway and the Amtrak rail lines, is compositionally simple, yet iconic and compelling. The three primary elements are the 150 foot high basketball topped spire, the 120 foot diameter sphere, and the intersecting 100,000 square foot horizontal, curved-roof exhibition pavilion that accommodates the entry, retail and lobby, and the north and south visitor parking plazas.

Integral to the site master plan, and connecting to downtown Springfield, is the pedestrian Walk of Fame, a tourist information center, a proposed Children's Museum and a bridge over the Amtrak rail lines to the Riverfront Park, completing the revitalization program.

Circulating through the retail arcades, the visitor arrives at the museum lobby with its "arena" ticket booth, and adjacent 200 seat movie/lecture theatre. Immediately east of the lobby is the glazed entry to the sphere, housing a regulation basketball court on the ground level. Elevators and perimeter exposed stairs access the second level containing the primary exhibition venues, and the third level balcony incorporating the members Honors Ring—suspended at the top of the spherical volume, overlooking the multi-imaged scoreboard and the center court below.

The primariness and singularity of the sphere as an exterior form is transformed on the interior by the complex intervention of elements that reveal the content and aspiration of the sport, as well as a varied and enriched architectural experience, memorializing the birthplace of basketball.

View north toward Springfield

View from northeast on I-91 | Entry lobby   Retail concourse toward entry lobby

Honors Ring from basketball court

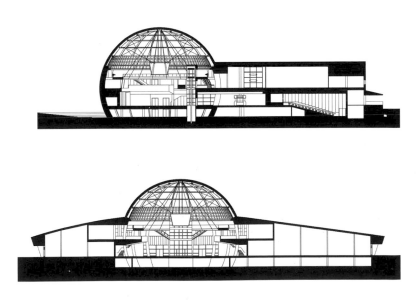

Detail view from second-level balcony | Cross section | Longitudinal section

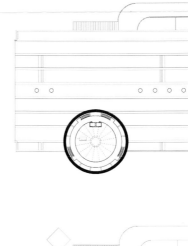

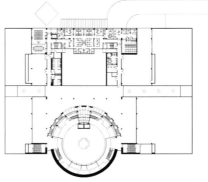

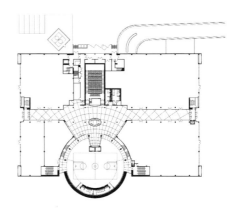

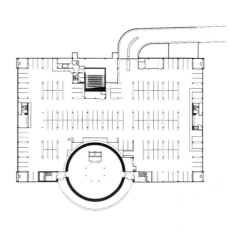

Detail view from second-level balcony | Exhibition gallery | View from balcony toward exhibition galleries | Third-, second-, ground-, and lower-level plans

Detail of stairs

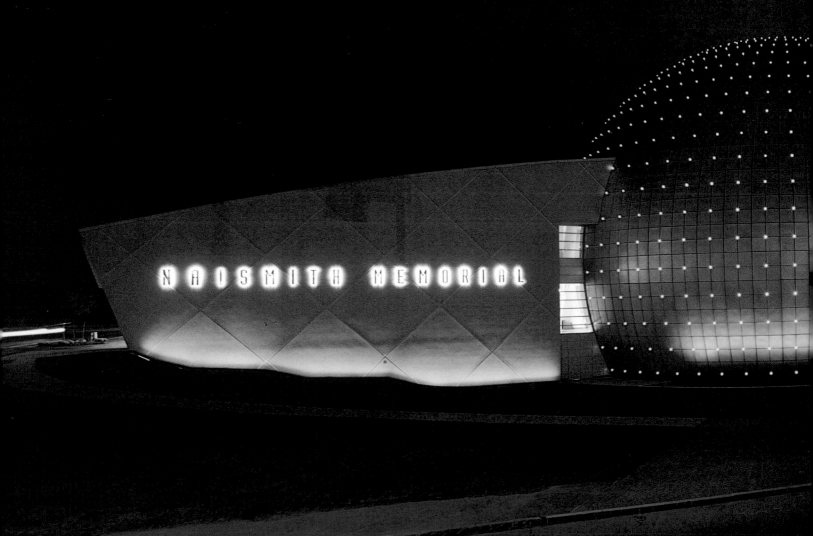

George E. Bello Center for Information and Technology

BRYANT COLLEGE   SMITHFIELD, RHODE ISLAND

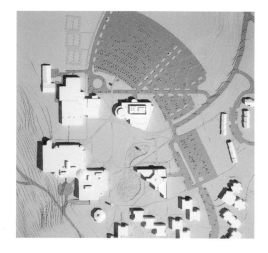

The design and realization of the new library transformed the entry image to the campus of this undergraduate business college and created a central pedestrian landscaped quadrangle that anchors the existing major buildings and establishes a new sense of place.

The primary element in the bi-nuclear composition is the two and a half story Grand Hall rotunda, which serves as both the main entry volume and the central campus meeting space, lounge, special events, and exhibition hall. Surrounding the rotunda on the second floor balcony/gallery are seminar/meeting rooms, classrooms and a fully integrated "mock Trading Room" for interactive learning and "real world" engagement.

The library, organized within a two story glass pavilion, overlooking the quad, contains a state-of-the-art electronic information services component, a double-height reading room, computer accessed, study carrols, stacks, classrooms, conference rooms, lounge, and administrative offices.

The building reflects the anticipated growth of the college as well as the understanding that architectural commitment raises the expectations and the aspirations of both the faculty and the student body.

Campus site model | View from south   Detail of south façade

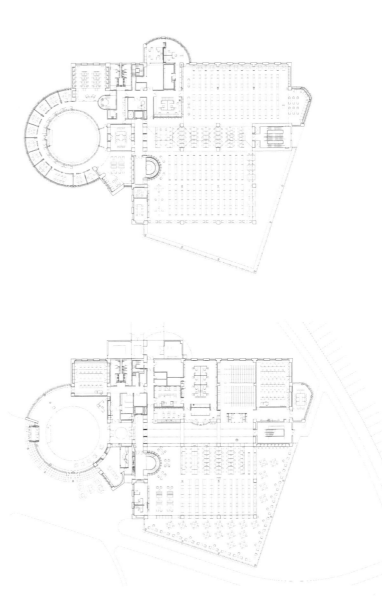

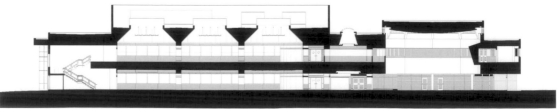

　　Main reading room and reference stacks　　|　　Longitudinal section

Periodical reading space | Main reading room | View from southeast (overleaf)

West façade

Louise Wells Cameron Art Museum

WILMINGTON, NORTH CAROLINA

The site for this new museum building, with its southern pine tree natural landscape, is exceptional for its history—with remains of trenches from the last Civil War battle in which the Union forces captured the city of Wilmington—and its location at the confluence of two major regional arteries. The building anchors the intersection, and establishes an architectural presence appropriate for the primary visual arts center in southeastern North Carolina.

The new 43,000 square foot facility is organized around a central double height circulation/exhibition galleria, which accommodates the entry, reception area, and museum store; sequentially accessing the permanent exhibition wing, configured as a sectionally modulated, chronologically sequenced series of interconnected galleries housing the museum's collection of 18th, 19th, and 20th century North Carolina art; the museum cafe and courtyard, designed as both social and temporary exhibition venue; the temporary exhibition wing with its three skylit flexible loft galleries; and at its end, the multi-use reception/lecture space.

Storage, service, and administration offices are housed in a two story [third] wing off the south side of the galleria.

The natural material palette of magnesium brick and zinc articulates a hierarchical massing, rendering the building as an abstract, provocative, contrapuntal, architectural collage imposed upon a natural rural site. The solid facade presents an ambiguous scale and establishes a sense of expectation and discovery that is revealed through the light filled, volumetric, modulated interior, which is further enriched by the art.

View from southwest

View from northeast | View from southeast

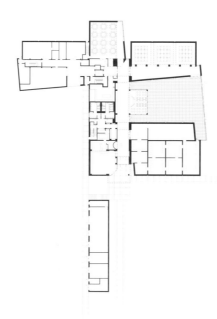

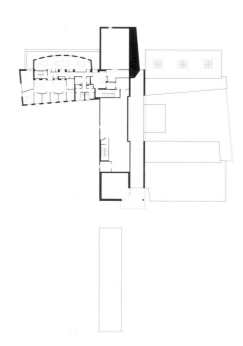

Main entry | Ground- and second-level plans

Entry galleria

Permanent exhibition galleries | Permanent exhibition galleries | Temporary exhibition galleries

Tangeman Student Center

UNIVERSITY OF CINCINATTI   CINCINATTI, OHIO

The new Student Center is part of a three building complex that includes the Recreation Center designed by Thom Mayne, and the Student Life Center, designed by Moore, Ruble, Yudell; intended to revitalize the existing central campus, defined by McMicken Hall Commons and Stadium.

The renovation and addition to the original 1935 brick, colonial building preserves the Greek Revival façade facing McMicken Commons; the slate gabled roof and cupula, a campus landmark; and the existing structure in which floors have been removed, creating a 90 foot high skylit central atrium space, from which the cupola is reviewed from the interior.

Surrounding the original brick structure is the new zinc and glass circulation addition, which negotiates the steeply sloping site and accommodates entries from the Commons, "Main Street" and Stadium levels.

The commons level to the original building accesses the student lounge, convenience store, and post office and connects to the new south addition housing on the same level and a restaurant and the campus bookstore.

The second level in the original structure houses the conference center, flexible meeting rooms, and the student senate. It connects to the new south building, which houses the 1,000 seat, multi-use Great Hall, overlooking the Stadium, and a roof terrace, over looking McMicken Commons.

The Main Street level is occupied by the food court surrounding a 200 seat movie theatre. The new south building houses the lower-level of the the bookstore, offices, and support space.

The Stadium entry level in the original structure houses the game rooms and lower movie theatre level. The south building contains loading docks and central campus kitchen.

The new zinc panel and shingle structures form a bi-nuclear, counterpointal composition that animates and contextually engages existing university buildings, outdoor spaces, and major circulation paths.

The collaboration with Mayne and Yurdell proved to be an inspiring, design intensive, critical dialogue, of the unique architectural collage/assemblage in a university community to visionary buildings.

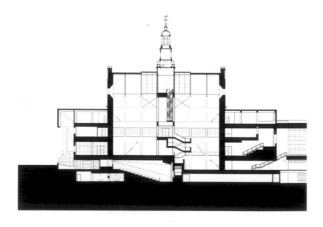

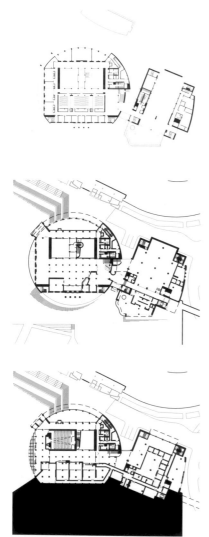

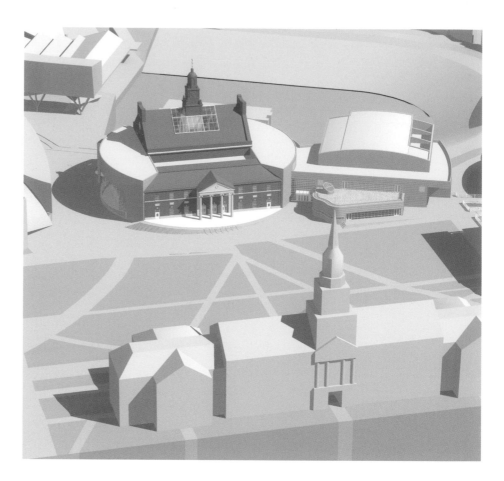

Second-, ground-, main street-, and lower ground-level plans | Aerial view of McMicken Commons from northwest | Existing aerial view of McMicken Commons from northwest

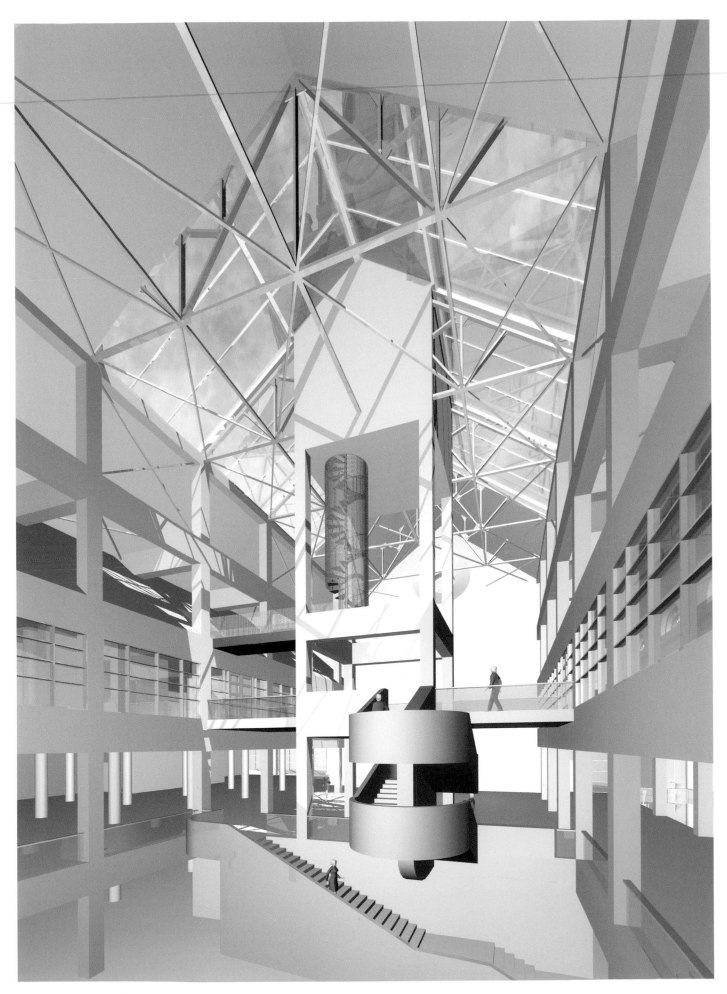

The Jewish Children's Museum

BROOKLYN, NEW YORK

Located on Brooklyn's Museum Row at Eastern Parkway and Kingston Avenue, the Jewish Children's Museum is at once an interactive, multi-media repository of cultural narratives and artifacts, as well as an urban community center that will encourage an understanding of Jewish history and culture through collective instruction and interaction.

The ground level, entered off the Eastern Parkway plaza, with its integral two story façade mural and corner sculpture, contains the lobby/reception, information space, restaurant, and museum store. The second level accommodates an orientation theatre, with retractable walls that expand the banquet/multi-use hall, and the art gallery. The third and fourth floors house the Jewish Life and History exhibits. The fifth floor contains museum office space and opens to a roof play terrace off the temporary exhibition gallery. The sixth floor contains executive offices and conference spaces. The lower level, entered separately off Kingston Avenue, yet interconnected to the lobby, houses a synagogue, theatre, library and computer classrooms.

The building, presents a compelling and memorable image, with its scale and compositional articulation, that is reinforced by its materiality—black magnesium brick, glass, and aluminum panels.

The six story high, two floor brick "table," capped by undulating steel mesh penthouse and bridging the four story aluminum and glass museum volume, offers an abstract, iconic presence that addresses an obligatory institutional scale, as well as mediating the existing residential neighborhood. The formal object/frame strategy proposed in the New York Public Library project as a renovation/addition is realized in this project as a new building.

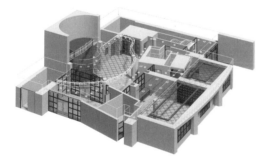

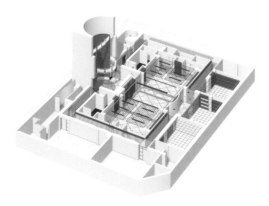

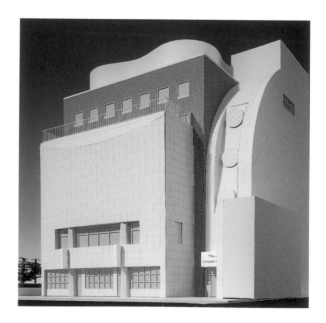

Second-, ground-, and lower-level plans | Northeast view from Kingston Avenue

Southeast view from Eastern Parkway

Aerial view from southeast

The new library, located on the eastern edge of Front Quad, is the initial structure in the college's new master plan. Its siting reinforces existing view corridors and pedestrian circulation routes, anchors an existing context and becomes the campus gateway building to the town.

The three story, 143,000 square foot modern facility reinterprets yet honors the historic Front Quad architecture, in its scale, articulation and referential materiality: Vermont marble, granite, and limestone.

Designed to become the campus intellectual and social center, the building will accommodate the college's state-of-the-art technology, expanding collection of traditional print material, including a "wired" study carrol for each of the college's students. The interior spaces fulfill the specific programmatic requirements within a varied and enriched volumetric vertical and horizontal spatial layering.

In support of the college's commitment to environmentally sensitive design, the project meets the highest rating from the Leadership in Environmental Design Standards, while fulfilling the simultaneous aspiration of establishing the library as the new campus icon.

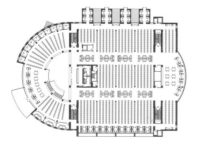

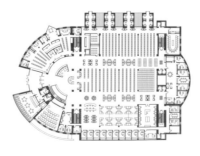

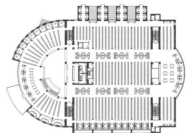

View from northeast | View from northwest | Second-, quad-, and street-level plans

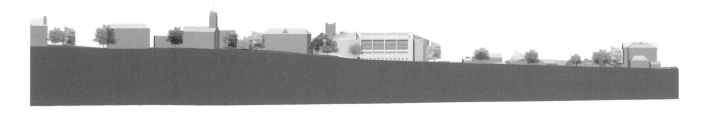

View of entry rotunda from upper-level reading room | South elevation   333

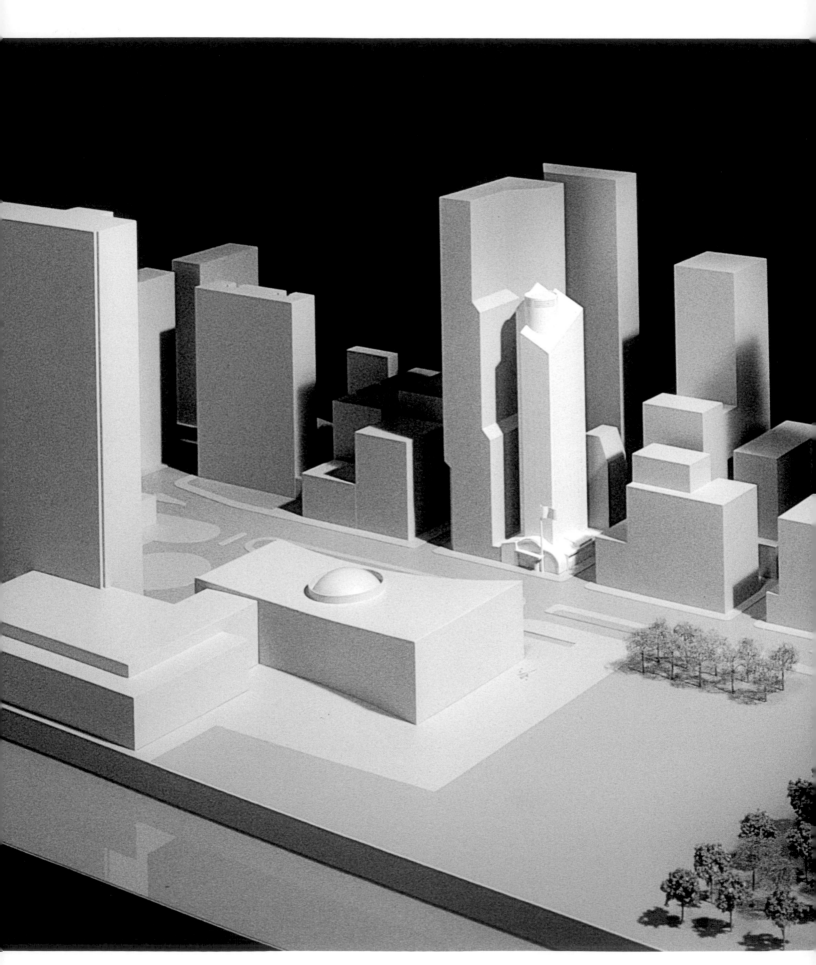

334 Aerial view from northeast

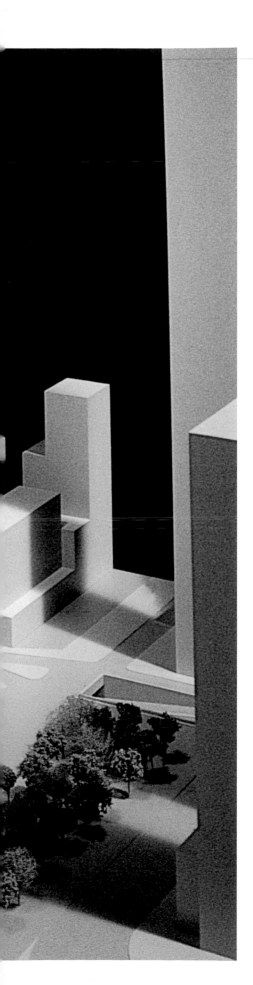

United States Mission to the United Nations

The Mission is located opposite the United Nations General Assembly Building on First Avenue and 45th Street, and is the only United States Embassy in America.

As a vertical building, the constraints were demanding, and afforded the opportunity to engage in an uniquely provocative, inventive, and discovery-oriented design process.

The challenge was to transcend the strict programmatic and technical requirements, including the maximum security and blast resistance criteria, in realizing an iconic tower that would be a compelling, representative architectural landmark to democracy and freedom.

The building refers to skyscraper precedents of base, middle and top, yet presents a unique topology of interlocking forms and materials that is initiated at street level with a glass enclosed, sculptural pavilion accommodating two entrances and adjacent granite clad security checkpoint volumes, which in turn access a split common elevator lobby in the base of the tower—one for the Mission and the other for the United States Information Agency and the Office of Foreign Missions.

The fenestration in the poured concrete, 22-story tower begin at the seventh floor, and become larger on each successive level, terminating in the seventy five foot high reception space at the top of the tower, which is the volumetric culmination of the zinc clad cylinder initially expressed at the buildings base.

The interlocking assemblage of forms and materials address the pedestrian scale at the street; a place defining object scale, juxtaposed to Kevin Roche's gridded mirror glass, U.N. Plaza Hotel; and the city scale, which is a unique, graphic, memorable silhouette.

Mid-Manhattan skyline from east   335

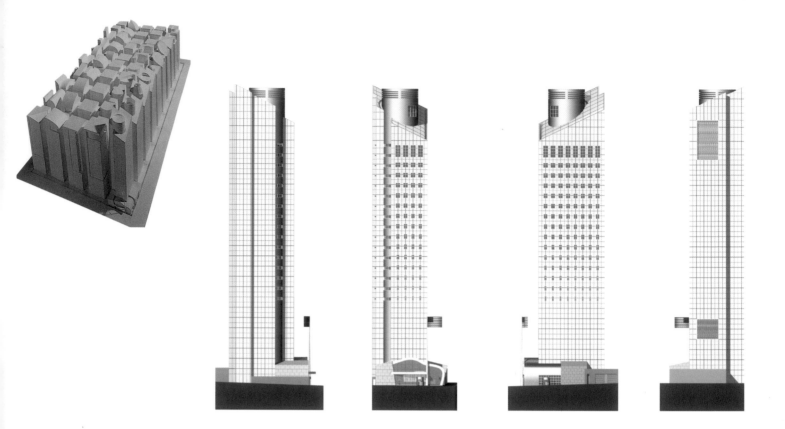

50 study models | South, east, north, and west elevations | View from northeast | View from southeast

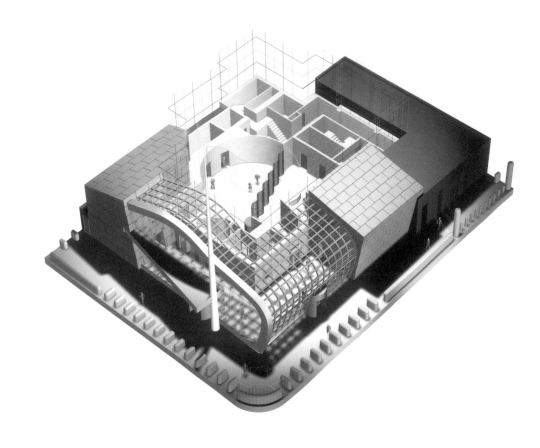

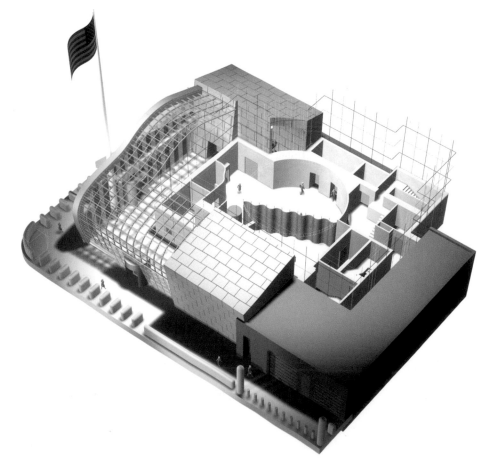

Ground-level axonometric from northeast | Ground-level axonometric from northwest

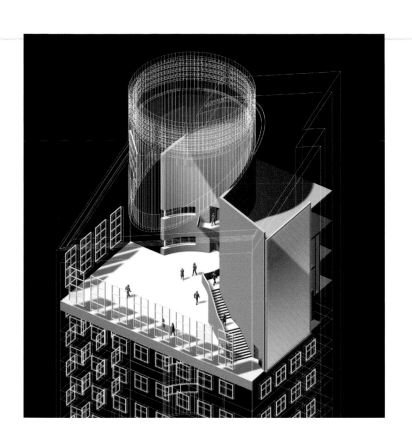

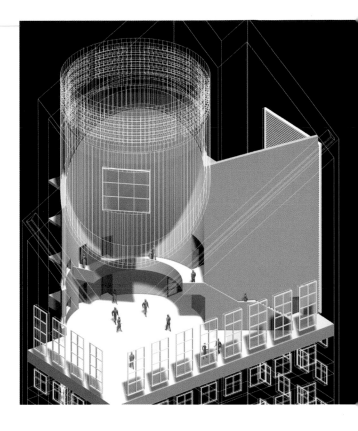

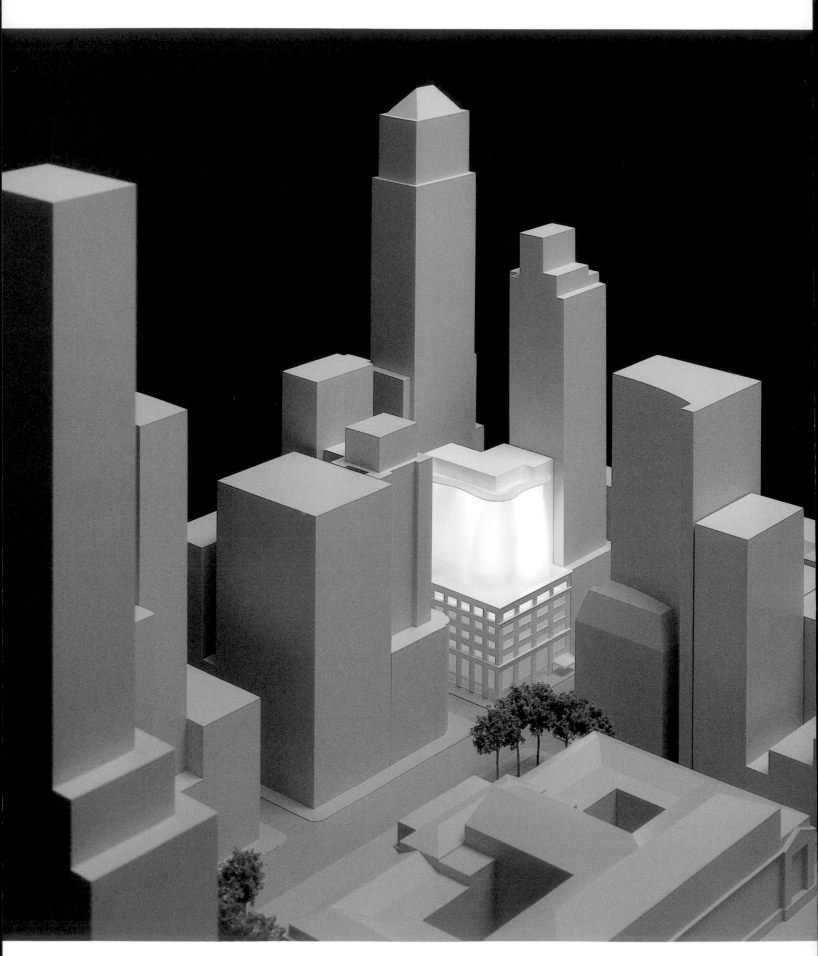

Aerial view from northwest

Mid-Manhattan Library Renovation and Expansion

THE NEW YORK PUBLIC LIBRARY   NEW YORK, NEW YORK

The current Mid-Manhattan Library occupies a prime location on Fifth Avenue and 40th Street in the former Arnold Constable building. The expansion will add an additional eight floors and 117,000 square feet for library service to the existing 139,000 square foot building; it will also create a 20,000 square foot ground floor and lower level retail space.

The expanded library will serve 8,000 people and offer state-of-the-art information technology including 300 computers, 100 laptops, and broad access to hundreds of electronic databases and training programs combining computer and library literacy.

Facilities will include five "Information Commons," one on each of five paired floors—Reference, Art, History and Social Sciences, and Periodicals—and an extensive popular library including multiple copies of the latest best-sellers, language books and literature in addition to biographies, mysteries, travel books and vacation guides, books on tape, videos, and current multi-media items.

The design maintains the existing building façades with structural modifications, retaining the contextual/urban reference, while re-imaging the limestone frame as a base and screen for a new, iconic intervention. Framed by the walls of adjacent taller buildings on both Fifth Avenue and Fortieth Street, the addition—an articulate, glass sheathed, sculptural, crystal volume—acts as a counterpart to the original buildings and anchors the corner, establishing a new modern "place marker" for the main New York Public Library/Bryant Park context.

The object/frame intervention refers to Whig Hall at Princeton University and the Guggenheim Museum, forth-eight blocks north on Fifth Avenue, with its counterpointal, modern, iconic presence adjacent to The Metropolitan Museum of Art.

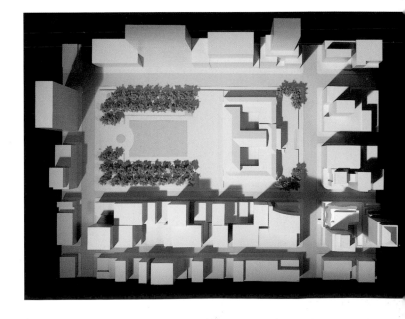

View from northwest | Site model   341

View from Fortieth Street above retail space | View from Fifth Avenue retail space

Section perspective of Fifth Avenue reading rooms 343

Fifth-, fourth-, third-, second-, ground-level plans | Ninth-, eighth-, seventh-, and sixth-level plans | Section   View of northwest from Fifth Avenue

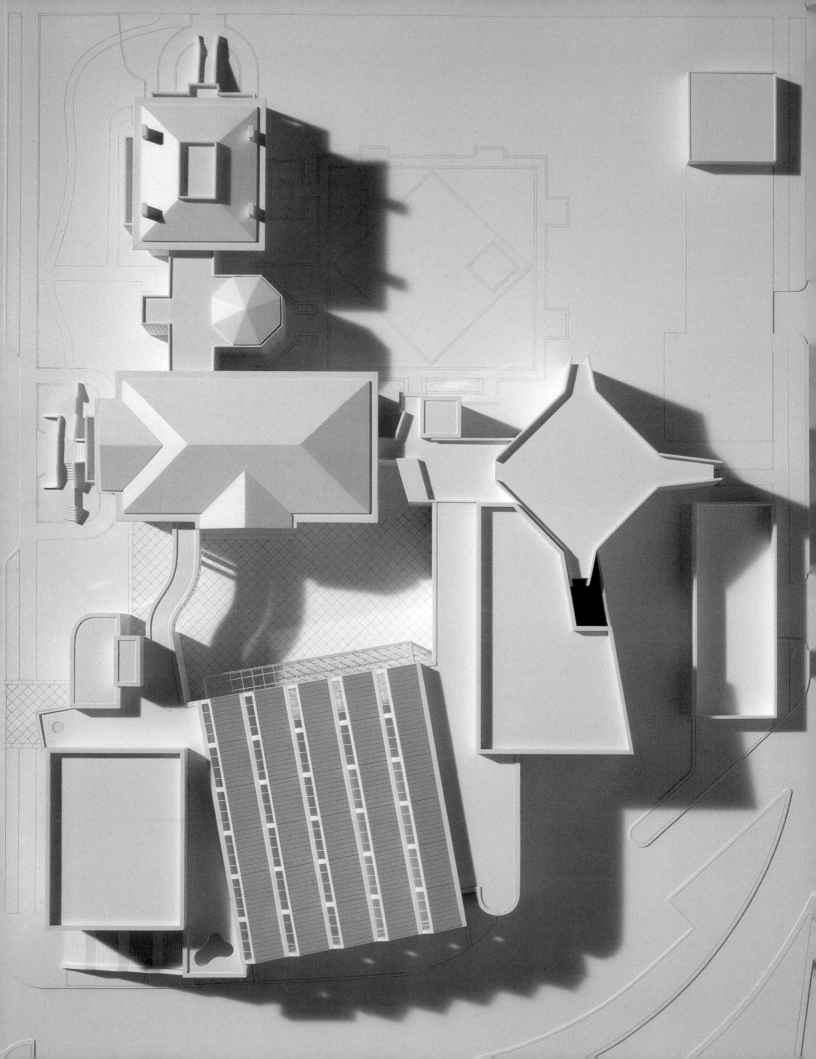

The Crocker Art Museum

SACRAMENTO, CALIFORNIA

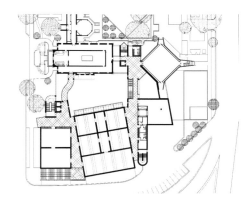

The Crocker Art Museum is a 45,000 square foot complex made up of the historic Crocker Art Gallery and family mansion and various later additions. Their current facilities are outgrown and inadequate. The goal is to create a world class facility through the re-programming, restoring and upgrading of existing facilities, and the expansion of the museum by 100,000 additional square feet.

The compositional strategy of the addition and renovation is to establish a new and unique iconic presence—a visually and physically dynamic frame for the existing complex, and a unified collaged image fronting the park.

The new addition is rotated on a due north/south axis, disengaging it from the existing orthogonal street grid and Crocker complex—which reinforces the counterpointal siting and massing—and confirming the non-replicatory strategy.

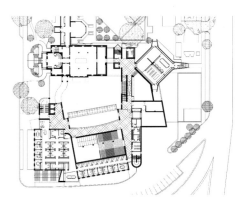

The ground floor contains a new entry off O Street, which accesses the museum store; reception desk; double height multi-use gallery/ reception space, which opens to a new courtyard; the cafe; public meeting rooms; auditorium; loading dock; and service support spaces.

Also accessible from the ground floor is a new connection/circulation space to the Herold Wing, which provides vertical and horizontal service and public access between the new addition and the existing buildings. The connection, which occurs on all three floors, re-façades the Herold Wing on the new courtyard side, creating a consistent architectural image for the space.

The second floor is occupied by the administrative offices, art storage spaces, with potential public viewing and access, as well as service spaces. On this level, the connection to the Herold Wing, facilitates access to the restored Ballroom and existing galleries.

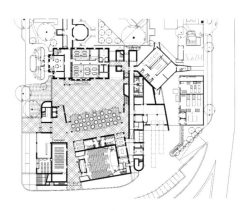

The third floor is occupied by the new suite of temporary exhibition galleries that afford maximum flexibility and installation variation. In addition to the Herold Wing connection, there is also a new bridge on the north end of the courtyard connecting the new gallery level to the Crocker Art Gallery, allowing for a continuous sequence. Thus integrating the entire complex, and affording, non-repetitive circulation options.

The material palette of zinc and limestone, is counterpointal to the painted Victorian Halianate façades of the historic buildings, which further enriches the architectural dialogue.

Site model | Longitudinal section | Third-, second-, and ground-level plans | 347

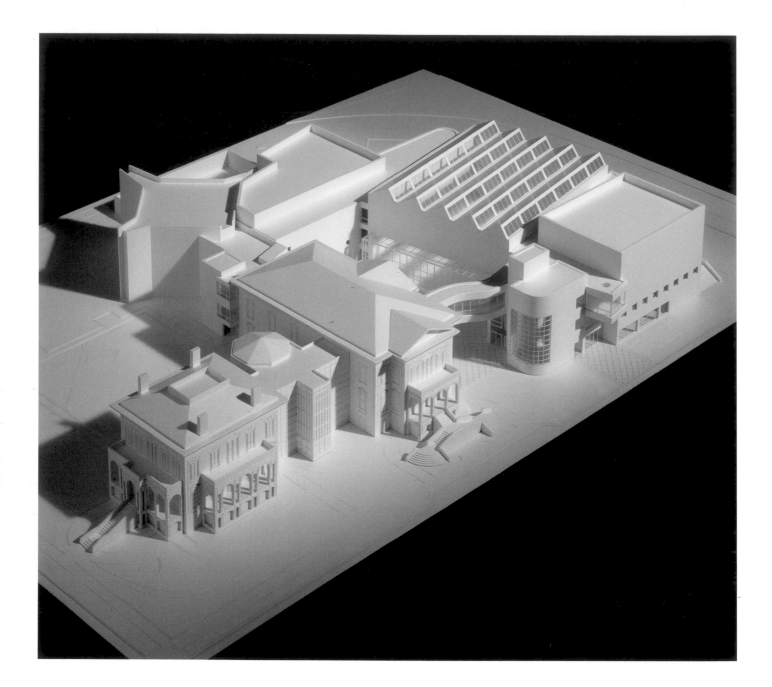

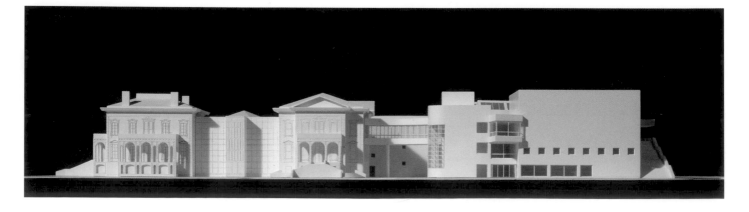

Aerial view from northeast | North façade

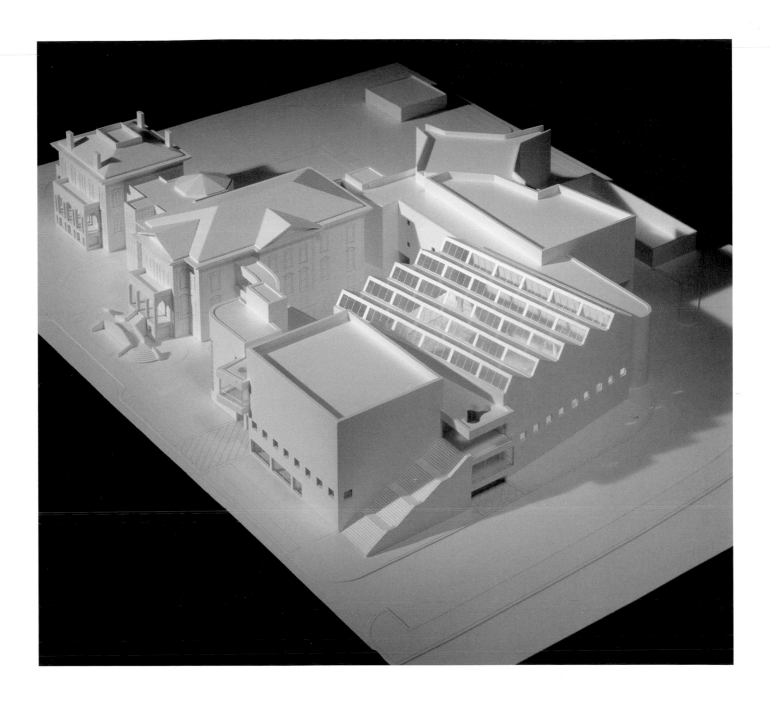

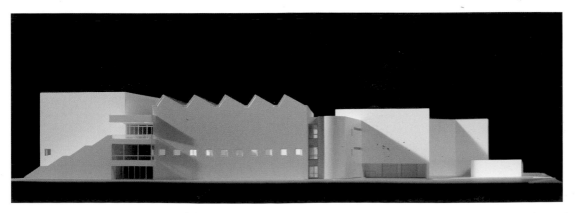

Buildings and Projects 1992 —

1992

Bonnet Creek Golf Clubhouse
WALT DISNEY WORLD
LAKE BUENA VISTA, FLORIDA

Joseph Ruocco, Edward Acari, Joseph Baker, Peter Guggenheimer, Richard Lanier, Loretta Leung

Center for the Arts
STATE UNIVERSITY OF NEW YORK AT BUFFALO
AMHERST, NEW YORK

Dirk Kramer, Philip Dordai, Jeffrey Bacon, Nancy Clayton, Rayme Kuniyuki,
Lee Ledbetter, Thomas Levering, Lilla Smith, Issac Swisher
Scaffidi and Moore Architects (Associate Architect)

Chen Residence
TAIPEI, TAIWAN

Jacob Alspector, Tsun-Kin Tam, Gregory Karn, Richard Lucas

Koppelman Apartment
NEW YORK, NEW YORK

Dirk Kramer, Lilla Smith, Jorge Castillo, Greg Epstein, Anthony Iovino, Karen Renick

Convention Center and Hotel (project)
EURO-DISNEY
MARNE-LA-VALLÉE, FRANCE

Joseph Ruocco, Greg Epstein, Richard Lucas, Juan Miro, Daniel Sullivan

Solomon R. Guggenheim Museum
Renovation and Addition
NEW YORK, NEW YORK

Jacob Alspector, Pierre Cantacuzene, Gregory Karn, Issac Swisher, Paul Aferiat, Pat Cheung,
Nancy Clayton, Marc DuBois, David Fratianne, Gerald Gendreau, Siamak Hariri, Anthony Iovino,
Dirk Kramer, Dan Madlansacay, David Mateer, Jeffery Murphy, Joseph Ruocco,
Gary Shoemaker, Robert Siegel, Irene Toroella, Alexandra Villegas, Peter Wiederspahn,
Ross Wimer, Stephen Yablon

Stadtportalhäuser (competition)
FRANKFURT AM MAIN, GERMANY

Jacob Alspector, Gregory Karn, Theodora Betow, Meta Brunzema, Pierre Cantacuzene, Barbara Krause, Richard Lanier, Daniel Sullivan, Elzbieta Skowronek, Frank Thaler

1993

The Capital Group, Inc. Offices WEST LOS ANGELES, CALIFORNIA

Dirk Kramer, Karen Renick, Peter Brooks, Meta Brunzema, Kathleen Byrne, Christopher Coe, Jay Levy, Lilla Smith

Oceanfront Residence
CALIFORNIA

Gerald Gendreau, Anthony Iovino, Nancy Clayton, Greg Epstein, Paul Mitchell

Golf Clubhouse
EURO-DISNEY
MARNE-LA-VALLÉE, FRANCE

Gerald Gendreau, Gregory Epstein, Mark Rylander
Rey-Grange & Jelensperger, RJ (Associate Architect)

Zumikon Residence
ZUMIKON, SWITZERLAND

Bruce Donnally, Nancy Clayton, Thomas Lewis, Sylvia Becker,
Pfister & Schiess Architekten (Associate Architect)

pp 12-23

1994

21 International Holdings, Inc.
NEW YORK, NEW YORK

Tsun-Kim Tam, Jay Levy, Lilla Smith, Daniel Sullivan, Scott Williams

717 Fifth Avenue
Corporate Interior and Lobby
NEW YORK, NEW YORK

Dirk Kramer, Stephen Forman, Joseph Hsu, Nicholas Martin,
Steven Mendelsohn, Jay Medok

EMI Records Group
Office Interiors
NEW YORK, NEW YORK

Tsun-Kin Tam, Gregory Karn, Daniel Sullivan, Peter Brooks

Eugenio Maria de Hostos Community College East Academic Complex
THE CITY UNIVERSITY OF NEW YORK   BRONX, NEW YORK

Jacob Alspector, Thomas Lekometros, Stephen Yablon, Jeffrey Bacon, Rustico Bernardo,
Karen Brenner, Pierre Cantacuzene, Nancy Clayton, Tom Demetrion, Marc DuBois, Ronald Ellis,
Steven Forman, Peter Franck, Gerald Gendreau, Anthony Iovino, Johannes Kastner,
Rayme Kuniyuki, Ming Leung, Dean Maltz, Paul Mitchell, J. Peter Pawlak, Joseph Ruocco,
Bryce Sanders, Thomas Savory, George Selkirk, Lilla Smith, Issac Swisher, Joseph Tanney,
Dickens van der Werff, Richard Velsor, Peter Wiederspahn, Ross Wimer

pp 182-187

1995

Master Plan and Three Academic Buildings
PITZER COLLEGE
CLAREMONT, CALIFORNIA

Gerald Gendreau, Gregory Karn, Thomas Lewis, Greg Epstein, Christine Marriott

Pace Wildenstein Gallery
BEVERLY HILLS, CALIFORNIA

Gerald Gendreau, Gregory Karn, Thomas Lewis, J. Peter Pawlak

pp 158-163

Pomerantz Apartment
NEW YORK, NEW YORK

Tsun-Kin Tam, Steven Forman, Gregory Karn, Antonio Gomes,
William Meyer, Daniel Sullivan

pp 24-29

Social Sciences Building and Super Computer Center
UNIVERSITY OF CALIFORNIA AT SAN DIEGO
LA JOLLA, CALIFORNIA

Bruce Donnally, Nancy Clayton, Richard Lanier, Peter Brooks, Thomas Lewis
Brown Gimber Rodriguez Park (Associate Architect)

pp 188-193

SONY Entertainment Headquarters
NEW YORK, NEW YORK

Richard Velsor, Bruce Donnally, Gustav Rosenlof, Stephen Yablon, Peter Brooks, Kathleen Byrne,
Steven Forman, Michael Girimonti, Pascal Jeambon, Barbara Krause, Richard Lanier, David Mateer,
J. Peter Pawlak, Tsun-Kin Tam, Frank Thaler

pp 134-139

Spielberg Apartment
NEW YORK, NEW YORK

Tsun-Kin Tam, Daniel Sullivan, Steven Forman, Antonio Gomes

1996

Baker Library (competition)
Graduate School of Business Administration
HARVARD UNIVERSITY
CAMBRIDGE, MASSACHUSETTS

Joseph Ruocco, Sean Flynn, Nelson Benavides, Wei Li Liu, Frank Visconti

Museum of Contemporary Art
NORTH MIAMI, FLORIDA

Tsun-Kin Tam, Daniel Sullivan, Gregory Karn, Frank Visconti
Gelabert Navia Architects (Associate Architect)

pp 202-205

The Science, Industry and Business Library
THE NEW YORK PUBLIC LIBRARY
NEW YORK, NEW YORK

Jacob Alspector, Sean Flynn, Issac Swisher, Ray Bakhshandegi, Wendy Burger, Oana Bretcanh,
Sandford Ferguson, Steven Forman, Michael Harshman, Phil Henshaw, Rebecca Iovino, Mark Hill,
Thomas Levering, Christine Marriott, Kira Leroy, Thomas Levering, David Mateer, Cheryl McQueen,
Mark Montalbano, Jeffrey Poorten, Elzbieta Skowronek, Daniel Sullivan

pp 194-201

1997

Citicorp Center
Tower, Plaza and Retail Atrium
NEW YORK, NEW YORK

Dirk Kramer, Susan Baggs, Joeseph Weiss, Victor Rodiriguez, Chang Hsin Lin,
Mark Montalbano, Lilla Smith

Hilltop Residence
AUSTIN, TEXAS

Gustav Rosenlof, Juan Miro, Lori Brown, Meta Brunzema, Sean Flynn,
Richard Lucas, J. Peter Pawlak

pp 92-107

Morgan Stanley World Headquarters
NEW YORK, NEW YORK

Thomas Levering, Richard Velsor, Stephen Yablon, Patricia Brett, Lance Hosey

pp 130-133

San Onofre Residence
PACIFIC PALISADES, CALIFORNIA

Gerald Gendreau, Greg Epstein, Joseph Hsu, J. Peter Pawlak, Sylvia Braun, Lori Brown

pp 30-41

The Henry Art Gallery
UNIVERSITY OF WASHINGTON
SEATTLE, WASHINGTON

Bruce Donnally, Nancy Clayton, Richard Lucas, William Meyer, John Reed
Loschky, Marquardt & Nesholm Architects (Associate Architect)

pp 216-229

Winnick Apartment
NEW YORK, NEW YORK

Celeste Umpierre, Thomas Lewis, David Yum

pp 42-47

1998

Mount Pleasant-Blythedale School
UNION FREE SCHOOL DISTRICT
VALHALLA, NEW YORK

Jacob Alspector, Joel Rosenberg, Issac Swisher, Sean Flynn, George Hauner, Alexander Zaretsky

The Herbert Irving Comprehensive Cancer Center
MEDICAL/SURGICAL ONCOLOGY CENTER
NEW YORK PRESBYTERIAN HOSPITAL
NEW YORK, NEW YORK

Thomas Levering, Cheryl McQueen, Wei Li Liu, Thomas Merton Wu

pp 146-149

The Herbert Irving Comprehensive Cancer Center
PEDIATRIC ONCOLOGY CENTER
NEW YORK PRESBYTERIAN HOSPITAL
NEW YORK, NEW YORK

Thomas Levering, Cheryl McQueen, Sarah Crozier, Yoko Murakami, Scott Skipworth

pp 150-153

James S. McDonnell Hall of Physics
PRINCETON UNIVERSITY
PRINCETON, NEW JERSEY

Nancy Clayton, Richard Kilbschon, Peter Brooks, Kang Chang, Bruce Donnally,
Christine Marriott, David Yum

pp 230-237

Levitt Center for University Advancement
UNIVERSITY OF IOWA
IOWA CITY, IOWA

Nancy Clayton, Bruce Donnally, Keith Goich, William Meyer, Kang Chang,
John Reed, Daniel Sullivan
Brooks Borg Skiles (Associate Architects)

pp 206-215

1999

Gymnasium/Fieldhouse
STATE UNIVERSITY OF NEW YORK AT ONEONTA
ONEONTA, NEW YORK

Joseph Ruocco, William Clark, Karen Renick, Ed Acari, Antonio Gomes, Keith Howie,
Loretta Leung, Stephen Sudak, Frank Thaler, David Yum

Ian Schrager Corporate Offices
NEW YORK, NEW YORK

Gerald Gendreau, Richard Klibschon, Victor Rodriguez

pp 164-167

Institute for Human Performance, Rehabilitation and Biomedical Research
STATE UNIVERSITY OF NEW YORK AT SYRACUSE
SYRACUSE, NEW YORK

William Clark, Thomas Levering, John Newman, Mark Rylander, Stephen Sudak, Patricia Bosch-Melendez, Peter Brooks, Sean Flynn, Antonio Gomes

pp 238-243

Lutheran Center
BALTIMORE, MARYLAND

Thomas Levering, Greg Epstein, Patrick Walsh
Marks Thomas Associates (Associate Architect)

Malibu Residence
MALIBU, CALIFORNIA

Dirk Kramer, Lilla Smith, Eva Frank, Mark Hill, Joseph Hsu, Christopher Liu, J. Peter Pawlak

pp 48-63

Nanyang Polytechnic
ANG MO KIO, SINGAPORE

Joseph Ruocco, Frank Visconti, Nelson Benavides, Peter Brooks, Greg Epstein, Mark Hill, Lance Hosey, Joseph Hsu, John Hunter, Jay Lampros, Richard Lanier, George Liaropoulos, Wei Li Liu, Gregory Luhan, Cheryl McQueen, Christine Straw, Frank Thaler
DP Architects, Singapore (Associate Architect)

pp 244-259

PepsiCo World Headquarters
Headquarters Master Plan and Facilities Upgrade
PURCHASE, NEW YORK

Thomas Levering, Patricia Bosch-Melendez, Cheryl McQueen, Luella Noles, Karen Renick, David Biagi, Timothy Butler, Sean Flynn, Scott Skipworth, Barry Yanku, Irene Yu

pp 140-145

The Ronald S. Lauder Foundation Offices
NEW YORK, NEW YORK

Joseph Ruocco, Nelson Benavides

pp 154-157

The Saint Vincents Comprehensive Cancer Center
Salick Health Care, Inc. Affiliate
NEW YORK, NEW YORK

Dirk Kramer, Eva Frank, Mark Hill, Melvin Aminoff, Anastasia Mastrogiorgis, Chang Hsiu Lin, Peter Juang, Jongmin Kim, Stephen O'Dell, Peter Ogman, Scott Skipworth, William Vinyard, Irene Yu

Salt Lake City Library (competition)
SALT LAKE CITY, UTAH

Jacob Alspector, Chen Ho-Hsu, Sora Kim, Takeshi Okada, William Vinyard

2000

The David Geffen Foundation Building
BEVERLY HILLS, CALIFORNIA

Dirk Kramer, Peter Ogman, Lilla Smith, Melvin Aminoff, Victoria Blau, Anastasia Mastrogiorgis, Peter Juang, Christopher Liu, Richard Lucas, Luella Noles, Juan Miro, Mark Montalbano, Joseph Ruocco, Barry Yanku

pp 168-173

The Graduate Center
THE CITY UNIVERSITY OF NEW YORK   NEW YORK, NEW YORK

Jacob Alspector, Steven Forman, Wendy Burger, Thomas Dahlquist , Thomas Florkewicz George Hauner, Robert Axten, Karen Brenner, Patricia Brett, Oana Bretcanu, Richard Cohen, Meghan Corwin, Greg Epstein, Sean Flynn, Antonio Gomes, John Hunter, Thomas Lekometros, Jeffrey Poorten, Victor Rodriguez, Joel Rosenberg, George Scarpidis, Rene Shiller, Scott Skipworth, Robin Tolud, Richard Velsor, William Vinyard, Patrick Walsh, Irene Yu, Alexander Zaretsky

pp 268-277

International Center of Photography
NEW YORK, NEW YORK

Celeste Umpierre, Joel Rosenberg, Elizabeth Rutherfurd

pp 278-283

Janklow Nesbit Offices
NEW YORK, NEW YORK

Joel Rosenberg, Sarah Crozier, Scott Skipworth

Maveron Tower
SEATTLE, WASHINGTON

Gerald Gendreau, Peter Ogman, Thomas Devanney
Associate Architect: Weber + Thompson Architects, plc

2001

Bel Air Residence
BEL AIR, CALIFORNIA

Gerald Gendreau, Eva Frank, Richard Klibschon, Meta Brunzema, Elaine Castro,
John Hunter, John Kim, Seungbom Roh

pp 108-127

FSU Library for Information Technology and Education
FERRIS STATE UNIVERSITY
BIG RAPIDS, MICHIGAN

Jacob Alspector, Sean Flynn, Takeshi Okada, Aurelie Paradiso,
Scott Skipworth, William Vinyard.

pp 284-293

Gymnasium Apartment
NEW YORK, NEW YORK

Gerald Gendreau, Eva Frank, Luella Noles, Timothy Butler, Elaine Castro,
J. Peter Pawlak, Scott Skipworth, Stephen Sudak

pp 64-71

Princeton Forrestal Center Office Building
PRINCETON UNIVERSITY
PRINCETON, NEW JERSEY

Joseph Ruocco, Melvin Aminoff, Dana Cho, Tom Delaney,
Yongseok John, Sora Kim, William Vinyard

Quadrangle
NEW YORK, NEW YORK

Barry Yanku, Thomas K. Dahlquist, Robert Morris III, Celeste Umpierre

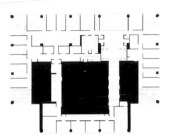

The Sackler Center for Arts Education
SOLOMON R. GUGGENHEIM MUSEUM
NEW YORK, NEW YORK

Jacob Alspector, Scott Skipworth, Ung-Joo Scott Lee, Robert Morris III, Krista Ninivaggi, Takeshi Okada, Victor Vetterlein

CPW Apartment
NEW YORK, NEW YORK

Kang Chang, Cordeila Fox-Waelle, Geoff O'Meara, Irene Yu

pp 80-85

Steel Loft
NEW YORK, NEW YORK

Kang Chang, Timothy Butler, Christopher Liu, Geoff O'Meara

pp 86-91

University Technology and Learning Complex
LAWRENCE TECHNOLOGICAL UNIVERSITY
SOUTHFIELD, MICHIGAN

Gerald Gendreau, Susan Baggs, Richard Klibschon, Sanuel Parker, Victor Rodriguez Neumann/Smith Architects (Associate Architect)

pp 260-267

2002

George E. Bello Center for Information and Technology
BRYANT COLLEGE
SMITHFIELD, RHODE ISLAND

Jacob Alspector, Steven Forman, Thomas Florkewicz, Kevin Brennan, William Clark, Richard Cohen, Sarah Crozier, Chien-Ho Hsu, Ho Jeong Kim, Ung-Joo Scott Lee, Brian McFarland, Krista Ninivaggi, Scott Skipworth, Victor Vetterlein, William Vinyard

pp 306-313

Louise Wells Cameron Art Museum
WILMINGTON, NORTH CAROLINA

Nancy Clayton, Cordelia Fox-Waelle, William Meyer, Anastasia Mastrogiorgis, Raymond Sutiono, Barry Yanku

pp 314-323

Naismith Memorial Basketball Hall of Fame
SPRINGFIELD, MASSACHUSETTS

Nancy Clayton, Barry Yanku, Cordelia Fox-Waelle, Brian McFarland, Takeshi Okada, Stephen Wilson
Bargmann Hendrie + Archetype (Associate Architect)

pp 294-305

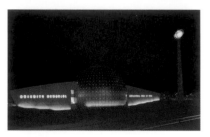

Miranova Penthouse
COLUMBUS, OHIO

Gregory Karn, J. Peter Pawlak, Victoria Blau, Elaine Castro, Eva Frank, Christine Marriott

pp 72-79

World Trade Center Competition
NEW YORK, NEW YORK

Gerald Gendreau, Scott Skipworth, Brian Arnold, Timothy Butler,
Clarisse Labro, Shannon Walsh, Barry Yanku, Yongseok John
Richard Meier & Partners (Associate Architect, Team Leader)
Steven Holl, Architect (Associate Architect)
Eisenman Architects(Associate Architect)

Akron-Summit County Public Library
2003
AKRON, OHIO

Jacob Alspector, Lilla Smith, Sean Flynn, Thomas Dahlquist, Jongmin Kim,
Cheryl McQueen, Takeshi Okada, Damon Strub, Kevin Wineinger, Victor Vetterlein

Belvedere Residence
BELVEDERE ISLAND, CALIFORNIA

Gerald Gendreau, Joseph Ruocco, Timothy Butler, Eva Frank,
Nelson Benavides, Elaine Castro

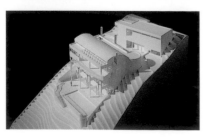

The Jewish Children's Museum
BROOKLYN, NEW YORK

Jacob Alspector, Joseph Ruocco, Mark Hill, Greg Epstein, Steve Rustow, Casey Sherman, Melvin Aminoff, Roberto Bannura, Linda Chung, Yongseok John, Peter Juang, Sora Kim, Cheryl McQueen, Zachary Moreland, Liana Sipelis, Stephen Wilson, Barry Yanku

pp 328-329

Maple Associates Ltd. Office Building
BEVERLY HILLS, CALIFORNIA

Dirk Kramer, Peter Ogman, Rayme Kuniyuki, Brian McFarland, Ed Acari, Chien-Ho Hsu, Peter Juang, Juan Miro, Warren Shaw, Lilla Smith, Stephen Wilson,

pp 174-179

Middlebury College Library
MIDDLEBURY COLLEGE
MIDDLEBURY, VERMONT

Joseph Ruocco, Mark Hill, Stephen Wilson, Roberto Bannura, Charlene Andreas, Kang Chang, Linda Chung, Cornilia Fox-Waelle, Sora Kim, Zachary Moreland, Casey Sherman, Liana Sipelis

pp 330-333

Tangeman Student Center
UNIVERSITY OF CINCINNATI
CINCINNATI, OHIO

Gregory Karn, Thomas Levering, Ivan Ziderov, Yongseok John, Seungwook Kim, Carl Weinbroer

pp 324-327

2004

Student Center and Academic Building
NEW JERSEY INSTITUTE OF TECHNOLOGY
NEWARK, NEW JERSEY

Thomas Levering, Thomas Devanney, Stephen Sudak, Yongseok John, Seungwook Kim, David McGullam, Robert Morris III, Carl Wienbroer, Ivan Zidarov

2005

Astor Place Condominiums
NEW YORK, NEW YORK

Joseph Ruocco, Yongseok John

1992
AIA New York Chapter
Distinguished Architecture Award
    Opel Residence
    Shelburne, VT

AIA New York Chapter
Distinguished Architecture Award
    Walt Disney World
    Contemporary Resort Convention Center
    Orlando, FL

1995
AIA New York Chapter
Design Award
    Solomon R. Guggenheim Museum
    Renovation and Addition
    New York, NY

Architectural Record
Record House
    Zumikon Residence
    Zumikon, Switzerland

1996
Architectural Record
Record Interiors
    New York Public Library
    Science, Industry and Business Library
    New York, NY

1997
AIA and ALA
Library Buildings Award
    New York Public Library
    Science, Industry and Business Library
    New York, NY

1999
AIA New York Chapter
Design Award
    University of Washington
    Henry Art Gallery
    Seattle, WA

AIA New Jersey Chapter
Design Award
    Princeton University
    James S. McDonnell Physics Building
    Princeton, NJ

2000
Buildings Magazine
2000 Modernization Awards
    The Graduate Center
    The City University of New York
    New York, NY

2001
AIA New York Chapter
Award of Merit
    Princeton University
    James S. McDonnell Physics Building
    Princeton, New Jersey

AIA New York Chapter
Award of Merit
    The Science, Industry and Business Library
    The New York Public Library
    New York, New York

Biographies

Charles Gwathmey, FAIA

Charles Gwathmey received his Master of Architecture degree in 1962 from Yale University, where he won both The William Wirt Winchester Fellowship as the outstanding graduate and a Fulbright Grant.

In the decades since, Mr. Gwathmey has been honored with the Brunner Prize from the American Academy of Arts and Letters in 1970 and election to the Academy in 1976. In 1983, he won the Medal of Honor from the New York Chapter of the American Institute of Architects and in 1985, received the first Yale Alumni Arts Award from the Yale School of Architecture. Three years later, the Guild Hall Academy of Arts awarded Mr. Gwathmey its Lifetime Achievement Medal in Visual Arts, followed in 1990 by a Lifetime Achievement Award from the New York State Society of Architects.

Mr. Gwathmey has served as President of the Board of Trustees for The Institute of Architecture and Urban Studies, as a trustee to The Cooper Union for the Advancement of Science and Art, and was elected a Fellow of the American Institute of Architects in 1981.

From 1965 through 1991, Mr. Gwathmey taught at Pratt Institute, Cooper Union for the Advancement of Science and Art, Princeton University, Columbia University, the University of Texas, and the University of California at Los Angeles. He was Davenport Professor (1983 and 1999) and Bishop Professor (1991) at Yale University, and the Eliot Noyes Visiting Professor at Harvard University (1985).

Robert Siegel, FAIA

Robert Siegel graduated from Pratt Institute with a Bachelor of Architecture degree in 1962 and received his Master of Architecture degree from Harvard University in 1963.

In 1983, the New York Chapter of the American Institute of Architects recognized his skill and leadership as an architect with its Medal of Honor. He received the Pratt Institute Centennial Alumni Award in Architecture in 1988, and, in 1990, accepted a Lifetime Achievement Award from the New York State Society of Architects. He was elected a Fellow of The American Institute of Architects in 1991.

Throughout his professional career, he has served as a design critic, juror, and lecturer at schools of architecture and for professional organizations. In 1983, he organized the Pratt Institute Student Intern Program within the Gwathmey Siegel office—part of his continuing interest in nurturing the skills of talented young architects.

Robert Siegel is Chairman of the Board of Trustees of Pratt Institute in New York City. Formerly he acted as Chairman of Pratt's Building and Grounds Committee. He was previously a member of the Harvard University Graduate School of Design Advisory Committee.

Gwathmey Siegel & Associates Architects

Founded in 1968, Gwathmey Siegel & Associates Architects is a New York-based architecture firm offering master planning, architectural, interior and product design services. The firm has completed over three hundred projects for educational, cultural, institutional, corporate, healthcare and private clients throughout the United States and abroad.

The 80-person firm has an international reputation for architectural excellence. It has received over 100 design awards, continuing recognition in the press, and inclusion in exhibitions and histories of contemporary architecture.

In 1982 Gwathmey Siegel & Associates became the youngest firm to receive the American Institute of Architects' highest honor—the Firm Award—for "approaching every project with a fresh eye, a meticulous attention to detail, a keen appreciation for environmental and economic concerns... and a strong belief in collaborative effort."

The Associates are senior architects who have collaborated with the partners extensively on a wide variety of projects. They lead the design discovery process, supervise the teams established for each project, are responsible for the selection and coordination of outside engineering and specialized consultants, and act as the liaison between the firm and its clients. The team's nucleus—the project architect and key staff—remains on the project team from its beginning through the design development and construction phases.

Charles Gwathmey and Robert Siegel are involved with the conceptual design direction and actively participate in the development process of each project which is managed on a daily basis by one of the Associates.

The firm gives the highest priority to the programmatic requirements of the client. This commitment, unencumbered by stylistic preconceptions, is matched by a rigorous attention to the budget and schedule.

Clients are valued collaborators in shaping project programs and determining design direction. Our approach is to synthesize from interaction and analysis, sensitive to the nuances of place and precedent.

Associates

Paul Aferiat
Jacob Alspector
William Clark
Nancy Clayton
Bruce Donnally
Eva Frank
Steven Forman
Gerald Gendreau
Mark Hill
Gregory Karn
Dirk Kramer
Thomas Lekometros
Thomas Levering
Peter Ogman
Gustav Rosenlof
Joseph Ruocco
Elzbieta Skowronek
Lilla Smith
Tsun-Kin Tarn
Richard Velsor
Stephen Wilson

Architects

Melvin Aminoff
Charlene Andreas
Edward Arcari
Robert Axten
Jeffrey Bacon
Susan Baggs
Roberto Bannura
Sylvia Becker
Nelson Benavides
Rustico Bernardo
Theodora Betow
David Biagi
Victoria Blau
Sebastien Boissard
Patricia Bosch-Melendez
Karen Brenner
Oana Bretcanh
Patricia Brett
Peter Brooks
Lori Brown
Meta Brunzema
Wendy Burger
Timothy Butler
Kathleen Byrne
Pierre Cantacuzene
Jorge Castillo
Kang Chang
Pat Cheung
Linda Chung
Christopher Coe
Richard Cohen
Jose Coriano
Lisa Crewey
Sarah Crozier
Christine Curran
Thomas Dahlquist
Tom Delaney
Tom Demetrion
Thomas Devanney
Susan Donegan
Philip Dordai
Marc DuBois
Ronald Ellis
Harry Elson
Greg Epstein
Sandford Ferguson
Thomas Florkewicz
Sean Flynn
Cordelia Fox-Waelle
Peter Franck
David Fratianne

Michael Girimonti
Keith Goich
Antonio Gomes
Peter Guggenheimer
Michael Harshman
George Hauner
Phil Henshaw
Lance Hosey
Keith Howie
Chien-Ho Hsu
Joseph Hsu
John Hunter
Anthony Iovino
Rebecca Iovino
Pascal Jeambon
Yongseok John
Peter Juang
Johannes Kastner
Ho Jeong Kim
John Kim
Jongmin Kim
Seungwook Kim
Sora Kim
Richard Klibschon
Barbara Krause
Rayme Kuniyuki
Hung Hua Lai
Richard Lanier
John Lampros
Lee Ledbetter
Judy Lee
Ung-Joo Scott Lee
Loretta Leung
Ming Leung
Frank Lew
Thomas Lewis
Jay Levy
George Liaropoulos
Chang Hsiu Lin
Christopher Liu
Wei Li Liu
Tze Tai Liu
Richard Lucas
Gregory Luhan
Dan Madlansacay
Dean Maltz
Richard Manna
Christine Marriott
Anastasia Mastrogiorgis
David Mateer
Jody Maybury
Brian McFarland
David McGullam
Cheryl McQueen
Jay Medok
Steven Mendelsohn
William Meyer
Jill Miller
Juan Miro
Paul Mitchell
Timothy Mock
Mark Montalbano
Adrienne Montare
Zachary Moreland
Robert Morris III
Yoko Murakami
Jeffery Murphy
David Must
John Newman
Luella Noles
Stephen O'Dell
Geoffrey O'Meara
Kevin O'Sullivan
Takeshi Okada
John Ostlund
Samuel Parker
Nicholas Pasanella
J. Peter Pawlak

Jeffrey Poorten
John Reed
Karen Henick
Joseph Rivera
Victor Rodriguez
Seungbom Roh
Joel Rosenberg
Steve Rustow
Elizabeth Rutherfurd
Mark Rylander
Bryce Sanders
Marta Sanders
Thomas Savory
George Scarpidis
Evan Schwartz
George Selkirk
Warren Shaw
Casey Sherman
Gary Shoemaker
Robert Siegel
Liana Sipelis
Scott Skipworth
Howard Stern
Damon Strub
Stephen Sudak
Daniel Sullivan
Raymond Sutiono
Isaac Swisher
Joseph Tanney
Frank Thaler
Elizabeth Tilney
Richard Tobias
Robin Tolud
Irene Toroella
Celeste Umpierre
Aimee Van Dyne
Victor Vetterlein
Alexandra Villegas
William Vinyard
Frank Visconti
Patrick Walsh
Joseph Weiss
Peter Wiederspahn
Carl Wienbroer
Scott Williams
Ross Wimer
Kevin Wineing,r
Thomas Merton Wu
Stephen Yablon
Barry Yanku
Irene Yu
David Yum
Alexander Zaretsky
Ivan Zidarov

Interns

Ray Bakhshandegi
Kevin Brennan
Sibylle Braun
Sandy Brunner
Dana Cho
William Corwin
Meghan Corwin
Frederico DelPriore
Laura Dunn
Nicole Fox
Isolde Franz
Paul Grabowski
Siamak Hariri
Beatrice Hunn
Brigham Keehner
Natalie Klinck
Matthew Krahe
Clarisse Labro
Dominik Lengyel
Kira Leroy

Mark Mancha
Nicholas Martin
Mark Mendlovsky
Jordan Murphy
Robert Nase
Krista Ninivaggi
Ben O'Meara
Sheryl Ostfield
Aurelie Paradiso
Amanda Reeser
Joseph Rivera
Brian Rodman
Michael Samra
Christy Anna Schesinger
Michelle Schutt-Eng
Gale Shir
Rene Shiller
Tim Sliger
Lindsay Smith
Greg Smith
Peter Syrett
Terry Thieli
Catherine Toulouse
Kevin Towey
Dickens van der Werff
Natalya Vidokle
Ulrich Von Ey
Christina Weppner
Anja Wodsak

Administration

Kathleen Agnoli
Patricia Alleyne
Brian Arnold
Alejandro Calderon
Adrienne Catropa
Elaine Castro
Paul Cheevers
Stephen Cheevers
Denise Czar
Beverly DeLeon
Andrea Dobbis
Russell Doolittle
Nancy Figured
Howard Foster
Lila Grealis
Lenore Goldberg
Kelly Hashimoto
Cesar Hernandez
Una Hinds Heron
Dennis Hoffmann
Sharon Iannone
Shelagh Jay
Tracey Kessler
Judy Leung
Caren Litherland
Marisol Lorenzo
Frederick Marciano
Rosemarie Mattiole
Jennifer McKnight
Carla Murray
Michael Murphy
Jennifer Pirwitz
Kim Ranier
Wilbur Rogers
Vanessa Ruff
Irene Shum
Shannon Spunaugle
Faustus St Marthe
Richard Staub
Kate Stirling
Shannon Walsh
Mark Vanderbeeken
Ruth Van Putten
Matthew Young
Laurent Wurstemberger

Photography Credits

all other photography courtesy of Gwathmey Siegel & Associates Architects

© Peter Aaron/Esto

Morgan Stanley World Headquarters
All photographs except p. 131 (top and bottom)

The Science, Industry and Business Library
THE NEW YORK PUBLIC LIBRARY
All photographs

Assassi Productions

Henry Art Gallery
UNIVERSITY OF WASHINGTON
All photographs except pp. 216, 220

Levitt Center for University Advancement
UNIVERSITY OF IOWA
Photographs on pp. 206/207, 207 (top), 208 (bottom), 209-211,
212 (bottom), 214 (top right)

Malibu Residence
Photographs on pp. 52 (top), 57 (bottom)

Pace Wildenstein Gallery
All photographs

San Onofre Residence
All photographs except p. 34 (top)

Social Sciences Building and Super Computer Center
UNIVERSITY OF CALIFORNIA SAN DIEGO
Photographs on pp. 188 (bottom), 188/189, 190/191, 192

Buildings and Projects
1993   Oceanfront Residence
1995   Pitzer College Master Plan
1997   San Onofre Residence
1997   Henry Art Gallery
1998   Levitt Center for University Advancement

Luc Boegly/Archipress

Buildings and Projects
1993   Golf Clubhouse

Tom Bonner

The David Geffen Foundation Building
All photographs

Maple Associates Ltd.
All photographs

Buildings and Projects
1993   The Capital Group, Inc. Offices

Steven Brooke Studios

Museum of Contemporary Art
All photographs except p. 203 (bottom)

Richard Bryant/Arcaid

Zumikon Residence
All photographs except p. 13 (bottom)

Tim Buchman

Louise Wells Cameron Art Museum
All photographs

Anita Calero

San Onofre Residence
Photograph on p. 34 (top)

© Scott Frances/Esto

Bel Air Residence
All photographs

George E. Bello Center for Information and Technology
BRYANT COLLEGE
All photographs except p. 306 (top)

Naismith Memorial Basketball Hall of Fame
All photographs except p. 294/295

Miranova Penthouse
All photographs

Buildings and Projects
2002   George E. Bello Center for Information and Technology
2002   Naismith Memorial Basketball Hall of Fame

© Jeff Goldberg/Esto

Morgan Stanley World Headquarters
Photographs on p. 131 (top and bottom)

East Academic Complex
Eugenio Maria de Hostos Community College
THE CITY UNIVERSITY OF NEW YORK
All photographs except p. 182 (bottom)

Introduction
Morgan Stanley World Headquarters (p. 9)

Introduction
Solomon R. Guggenheim Museum Renovation and Addition

Buildings and Projects
1992   Center for the Arts
1992   Solomon R. Guggenheim
        Museum Renovation and Addition
1994   East Academic Complex
        Eugenio Maria de Hostos Community College
1997   Citicorp Center Tower, Plaza and Retail Atrium
1997   Morgan Stanley World Headquarters
1999   The Saint Vincents Comprehensive Cancer Center
        Salick Health Care, Inc. Affiliate

Hewitt/Garrsion

Social Sciences Building and Super Computer Center
UNIVERSITY OF CALIFORNIA SAN DIEGO
Photographs on pp. 188 (top), 191 (top), 192/193 (top)

Buildings and Projects
1995   Social Sciences Building and Super Computer Center

Elliot Kaufman

Buildings and Projects
1992   Bonnet Creek Golf Clubhouse

James Langone

Naismith Memorial Basketball Hall of Fame
Photograph on p. 294/295

Albert Lim KS

Nanyang Polytechnic
Photographs on pp. 244 (top), 248, 251-253, 256 (bottom), 256-259

Bill Lyons/Catalyst Studios

Institute for Human Performance, Rehabilitation
and Biomedical Research
STATE UNIVERSITY OF NEW YORK AT SYRACUSE
All photographs

Norman McGrath

Introduction
Princeton University, Whig Hall (p. 9)

James S. McDonnell Hall
PRINCETON UNIVERSITY
All photographs

Buildings and Projects
1998   Mount Pleasant-Blythedale School

Justin Maconochie

FSU Library for Information, Technology and Education
FERRIS STATE UNIVERSITY
All photographs

University Technology and Learning Complex
LAWRENCE TECHNOLOGICAL UNIVERSITY
All photographs

Mancia/Bodmer

Zumikon Residence
Photograph on p. 13 (bottom)

Michael Moran

The Lauder Foundation Offiice
All photographs

Ian Schrager Corporate Offiice
All photographs

J. Murphy

Introduction
SUNY Purchase (p. 9)

Richard Payne

Hilltop Residence
All photographs

Levitt Center for University Advancement
UNIVERSITY OF IOWA
Photographs on pp. 207 (bottom), 208 (top), 212 (top), 212/213,
214 (top left and bottom), 215

Introduction
First City Bank (p. 8)
Columbia University (p. 9)

© Jock Pottle/Esto

The Crocker Art Museum
All photographs

George E. Bello Center for Information and Technology
BRYANT COLLEGE
Photograph on p. 306 (top)

The Jewish Children's Museum
All photographs

Middlebury College Library
MIDDLEBURY COLLEGE
All photographs

Mid-Manhattan Library Renovation and Expansion
THE NEW YORK PUBLIC LIBRARY
All photographs

University Technology and Learning Complex
LAWRENCE TECHNOLOGICAL UNIVERSITY
Photograph on pp. 260

United States Mission to the United Nations
All photographs

Buildings and Projects
1992   Chen Residence
1992   Convention Center and Hotel
1992   Stadtportalhäuser
2000   Maveron Tower
2003   Akron-Summit County Public Library
2003   Belvedere Residence
2006   Allen County Public Library Addition and Renovation
2006   Villa at Jumeira

Erhard Pfeiffer

Malibu Residence
All photographs except pp. 52 (top), 57 (bottom)

Nanyang Polytechnic
Photographs on pp. 244/245, 246-247, 249, 250/251, 254-255,
256/257, 257 (bottom)

Buildings and Projects
1999   Malibu Residence
1999   Nanyang Polytechnic

Durston Saylor

Sony Entertainment Headquarters
All photographs except pp. 134-135

Buildings and Projects
1992   Koppelman Apartment
1994   21 International Holdings, Inc.

Roberto Shezen
Introduction
Gwathmey Residence and Studio (p. 9)

© David Sundberg/Esto
Buildings and Projects
1999   Gymnasium/Fieldhouse

Luca Vignelli
Biographies
Charles Gwathmey, Robert Siegel (p. 364)

Paul Warchol
The Graduate Center
THE CITY UNIVERSITY OF NEW YORK
All photographs

Gymnasium Apartment
All photographs

The Herbert Irving Cancer Center
NEW YORK PRESBYTERIAN HOSPITAL
All photographs

International Center of Photography
All photographs

PepsiCo World Headquarters
All photographs

Pomerantz Apartment
All photographs

Steel Loft
All photographs

Winnick Apartment
All photographs

Buildings and Projects
1994   717 Fifth Avenue Corporate Interior and Lobby
1994   EMI Records Group Office Interiors
2000   Janklow Nesbit Offices

Christopher Weil
CPW Apartment
All photographs